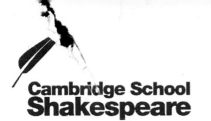

Cambridge School
Shakespeare

*Annie
Macaulay*

The Merchant of Venice

Edited by Jonathan Morris and Robert Smith

Series Editor: Rex Gibson
Director, Shakespeare and Schools Project

CAMBRIDGE
UNIVERSITY PRESS

CAMBRIDGE UNIVERSITY PRESS
Cambridge, New York, Melbourne, Madrid, Cape Town, Singapore,
São Paulo, Delhi, Dubai, Tokyo, Mexico City

Cambridge University Press
The Edinburgh Building, Cambridge CB2 8RU, UK

www.cambridge.org
Information on this title: www.cambridge.org/9780521618755

Commentary and notes © Cambridge University Press 1992, 2005
Text © Cambridge University Press 1987, 2005

First published 1992
Second edition 2005
7th printing 2010

Printed in the United Kingdom by Latimer Trend

A catalogue record for this publication is available from the British Library

ISBN 978-0-521-61875-5 Paperback

ACKNOWLEDGEMENTS
Thanks are due to the following for permission to reproduce illustrations:
Cover, v, vi, vii, ix, x, xi, xii, 8, 31, 73, 113, 120, 165, 175*tl*, 178, 190, 192, 193*t*,
195*b*, Donald Cooper/Photostage; 4, © Ancient Art & Architecture Collection Ltd; 28,
175*tr*, *bl*, 191, by permission of the Shakespeare Birthplace Trust; 36, Joe Cocks Studio
Collection © Shakespeare Birthplace Trust; 48, 68, Terence Hoyles; 58, 143, Michael
Le Poer Trench; 84, Ivan Kyncl; 142, 188, from *Der gelbe Stern* by G. Schoenberner,
Rütter & Loening Verlag, Hamburg/© Kongress Verlag, Berlin/photo Wiener Library,
London; 175*cl*, Henry Irving as Shylock, V&A Images/Victoria and Albert Museum;
175*br*, photograph by Anthony Crickmay, V&A Images/Victoria and Albert Museum;
193*b*, Richard Feldman; 195*t*, John Tramper.

Cover design by Smith

Contents

List of characters	1
The Merchant of Venice	3
What is the play about?	166
Characters	171
The language of *The Merchant of Venice*	180
History and the Jews	186
The Merchant of Venice in performance	189
William Shakespeare	196

Cambridge School
Shakespeare

This edition of *The Merchant of Venice* is part of the **Cambridge School Shakespeare** series. Like every other play in the series, it has been specially prepared to help all students in schools and colleges.

This *Merchant of Venice* aims to be different from other editions of the play. It invites you to bring the play to life in your classroom, hall or drama studio through enjoyable activities that will increase your understanding. Actors have created their different interpretations of the play over the centuries. Similarly, you are encouraged to make up your own mind about *The Merchant of Venice*, rather than having someone else's interpretation handed down to you.

Cambridge School Shakespeare does not offer you a cut-down or simplified version of the play. This is Shakespeare's language, filled with imaginative possibilities. You will find on every left-hand page: a summary of the action, an explanation of unfamiliar words, a choice of activities on Shakespeare's language, characters and stories.

Between each act and in the pages at the end of the play, you will find notes, illustrations and activities. These will help to increase your understanding of the whole play.

There are a large number of activities to give you the widest choice to suit your own particular needs. Please don't think you have to do every one. Choose the activities that will help you most.

This edition will be of value to you whether you are studying for an examination, reading for pleasure, or thinking of putting on the play to entertain others. You can work on the activities on your own or in groups. Many of the activities suggest a particular group size, but don't be afraid to make up larger or smaller groups to suit your own purposes.

Although you are invited to treat *The Merchant of Venice* as a play, you don't need special dramatic or theatrical skills to do the activities. By choosing your activities, and by exploring and experimenting, you can make your own interpretations of Shakespeare's language, characters and stories. Whatever you do, remember that Shakespeare wrote his plays to be acted, watched and enjoyed.

Rex Gibson

This edition of *The Merchant of Venice* uses the text of the play established by Elizabeth Story Donno in **The New Cambridge Shakespeare**.

Antonio (left), the Merchant of Venice, arranges to borrow money from Shylock to enable his friend Bassanio to woo Portia. Antonio agrees to forfeit a pound of his flesh if he cannot repay the loan.

But Shylock, a Jew, is despised by the Christians who seize any opportunity to torment him. Their cruel treatment of him bodes ill for Antonio.

'the will of a living daughter curbed by the will of a dead father' – Portia (left), the wealthy mistress of nearby Belmont, explains to her maid, Nerissa, the restrictions placed upon her by her dead father's will. She must marry the man who solves the riddle set by her father about three caskets of gold, silver and lead.

Two of Portia's suitors try to work out the correct answer to the riddle set by her father. Whoever opens the casket containing Portia's portrait will win her hand in marriage. The first two suitors fail the test.

'Our house is hell' – Shylock's daughter, Jessica, loves a Christian man, Lorenzo, and plans to elope with him. She is relieved to escape from her home. Jessica's betrayal of her father precipitates his distress and fury. He determines to enforce his 'bond' – a pound of Antonio's flesh.

'Hath not a Jew eyes?' Shylock, bitter over the loss of his daughter, and his hostile treatment by the Christians, stresses the common humanity of all men. But he also settles on a course of revenge against the financially vulnerable Antonio.

Bassanio, wary of fine but deceptive appearance, chooses the correct, lead casket and claims his reward – Portia: 'Myself, and what is mine, to you and yours / Is now converted.'

Shylock resolves to take the financially stricken Antonio to court to pursue the full terms of the contract: 'The pound of flesh which I demand of him / Is dearly bought; 'tis mine, and I will have it.'

The court assembles to judge if Shylock can cut the pound of flesh from Antonio. All productions have to decide how to stage this tense and dramatic scene.

Portia, disguised as the legal expert Balthazar, appears at the trial to act for Antonio. She advocates the need to show mercy: 'The quality of mercy is not strained . . .'

'You must prepare your bosom for his knife' – Shylock is triumphant, anticipating the shedding of Antonio's blood.

'Tarry a little . . .' – At the last moment, Portia reveals a loophole in the contract which releases Antonio from the grip of death. Shylock leaves the court a broken man.

The final act moves back to Belmont to focus on reconciliation and harmony. Lorenzo and Jessica are joined by Bassanio and Portia, and Nerissa and her recently acquired husband, Gratiano. Antonio, alone, reflects on the events of the play.

List of characters

Venice

Christians

THE DUKE OF VENICE

BASSANIO, a lord
ANTONIO, a merchant
SOLANIO
SALARINO — Friends of
GRATIANO } Antonio and
SALERIO — Bassanio
LORENZO

LANCELOT GOBBO, servant first
to Shylock, then to Bassanio
GOBBO, his father
STEPHANO, a messenger
JAILER
LEONARDO, servant of Bassanio
SERVINGMAN, employed by
Antonio
MAGNIFICOES OF VENICE
COURT OFFICIALS

Jews

SHYLOCK, a rich money-lender
JESSICA, his daughter
TUBAL, his friend

Belmont

Portia's household

PORTIA, a rich heiress
NERISSA, her lady-in-waiting
BALTHAZAR, her servant
SERVINGMAN
MESSENGER

Portia's suitors

THE PRINCE OF MOROCCO
THE PRINCE OF ARRAGON

The action of the play takes place in Venice and Belmont.

Antonio says he does not know what causes his sadness. Salarino and Solanio suggest that he is worried about the safety of his ships, in which he has invested so much money.

---

1 Antonio's sadness – why?

The opening line of the play quickly establishes that Antonio, the Merchant of Venice, is in melancholy mood. But he is also puzzled by why he is sad. As the first scene unfolds, compile a list of the possible reasons for his sadness. At the end of the scene, the whole class pools its ideas.

2 Where do they meet? Set the scene (in pairs)

Shakespeare left no stage directions to show the exact location of each scene. On the Elizabethan stage the action flowed swiftly from scene to scene without the aid of an elaborate set. Since Shakespeare's day, each editor of the play, and each director of a stage production, takes decisions about whether they will indicate precise locations. So try your hand at scene-setting. Decide on a suitable place in Venice for the three friends' meeting. Perhaps they meet in a house or an office, or in a public place such as a bar, a café or the Stock Exchange. Give reasons for your choice.

3 Add actions to words (in pairs)

In lines 15–22 Solanio describes nervously waiting for the safe outcome of a trade deal involving transport by sea. What gestures or actions would you suggest to an actor to accompany his speech? Take turns to speak the lines, adding actions. Show your ideas to the rest of the class. The following explanations will help you:

'Plucking . . . wind' – throwing grass in the air to find the
    direction of the wind
'Piring' – looking closely at
'roads'– anchorages

---

sooth truth
to learn ignorant
And . . . myself sadness has made
  me so absent-minded that I hardly
  know who I am
argosies merchant ships
portly stately

signors gentlemen
burghers important citizens
pageants processions
Do . . . traffickers look down on small
  boats
do them reverence show them
  respect

The Merchant of Venice

Act 1 Scene 1
Venice

Enter ANTONIO, SALARINO, and SOLANIO

ANTONIO In sooth I know not why I am so sad.
      It wearies me, you say it wearies you;
      But how I caught it, found it, or came by it,
      What stuff 'tis made of, whereof it is born,
      I am to learn.   5
      And such a want-wit sadness makes of me,
      That I have much ado to know myself.
SALARINO Your mind is tossing on the ocean,
      There where your argosies with portly sail
      Like signors and rich burghers on the flood,   10
      Or as it were the pageants of the sea,
      Do overpeer the petty traffickers
      That curtsey to them, do them reverence,
      As they fly by them with their woven wings.
SOLANIO Believe me, sir, had I such venture forth,   15
      The better part of my affections would
      Be with my hopes abroad. I should be still
      Plucking the grass to know where sits the wind,
      Piring in maps for ports, and piers, and roads;
      And every object that might make me fear   20
      Misfortune to my ventures, out of doubt
      Would make me sad.

Antonio says he is not worried about business matters. He has invested his money in several ships. That is much safer than relying on only one. He's not in love either!

1 A trader's journal

Salarino says that if he were in Antonio's situation, everything he did or saw would constantly remind him of what disasters might happen to his ships. Even blowing his soup to cool it would make him think of tempests. Lines 22–36 are full of images of calamity at sea.

Using ideas from lines 22–36, the picture below and your own ideas, write a diary entry for one of the Venetian merchants who is awaiting the safe arrival of some valuable goods.

2 I'm not in love . . .

Antonio is quick to deny that he is in love ('Fie, fie!'). What might this suggest about his attitude to women? Experiment with different ways of delivering this short line in order to show Antonio's troubled emotional state.

---

wealthy Andrew   the *San Andrés* (St Andrew), a valuable Spanish ship captured by the English in 1596
Vailing . . . top   bowing down her mainmast

holy . . . stone   the font
Janus   a Roman god who faced in two opposite directions
Nestor   a Greek king, famed for his seriousness

SALARINO   My wind cooling my broth
          Would blow me to an ague when I thought
          What harm a wind too great might do at sea.
          I should not see the sandy hourglass run   25
          But I should think of shallows and of flats,
          And see my wealthy Andrew docked in sand,
          Vailing her high top lower than her ribs
          To kiss her burial. Should I go to church
          And see the holy edifice of stone   30
          And not bethink me straight of dangerous rocks,
          Which touching but my gentle vessel's side
          Would scatter all her spices on the stream,
          Enrobe the roaring waters with my silks,
          And (in a word) but even now worth this,   35
          And now worth nothing? Shall I have the thought
          To think on this, and shall I lack the thought
          That such a thing bechanced would make me sad?
          But tell not me: I know Antonio
          Is sad to think upon his merchandise.   40
ANTONIO Believe me, no. I thank my fortune for it,
          My ventures are not in one bottom trusted,
          Nor to one place; nor is my whole estate
          Upon the fortune of this present year:
          Therefore my merchandise makes me not sad.   45
SOLANIO Why then, you are in love.
ANTONIO   Fie, fie!
SOLANIO Not in love neither? Then let us say you are sad
          Because you are not merry; and 'twere as easy
          For you to laugh and leap, and say you are merry
          Because you are not sad. Now by two-headed Janus,   50
          Nature hath framed strange fellows in her time:
          Some that will evermore peep through their eyes,
          And laugh like parrots at a bagpiper;
          And other of such vinegar aspèct,
          That they'll not show their teeth in way of smile   55
          Though Nestor swear the jest be laughable.

More friends arrive. One of them, Gratiano, comments on how careworn Antonio has become. He recommends laughter over misery and warns against false seriousness.

---

1 Friends? Or . . .? (in groups of three)

The entrance of Bassanio and his two friends, Lorenzo and Gratiano, can be used to change the mood of the scene. Although briefly there are six men on stage, Solanio and Salarino decide to leave when the others arrive. What prompts their departure? Are there tensions between these two groups of friends?

a Take parts and read aloud lines 57–68 in different ways. Are these words as friendly and polite as they appear?

b What have Solanio and Salarino made of Antonio? Either write their thoughts on taking their leave of him, or improvise a later conversation between them.

2 All the world's a stage – two players (in pairs)

Antonio's lines 77–9 echo well-known words from Act 2 Scene 7 of Shakespeare's *As You Like It*:

> All the world's a stage,
> And all the men and women merely players:
> They have their exits and their entrances
> And one man in his time plays many parts

a Talk together about what Antonio's lines reveal about him and his view of life.

b Gratiano makes it clear that the part he wants to 'play' is 'the Fool' (line 79). His long speech satirises the ways in which many Elizabethan men pretend to be what they are not. Take turns to speak lines 88–99 and then talk together about what they show of Gratiano's attitudes and values.

Your . . . regard you're a good friend
strange unfriendly
We'll . . . yours our time is yours
You . . . world you care too much about what people think
And . . . groans I'd rather cheer myself up with drink than weaken my heart with sighs and being miserable
Sit . . . alabaster be like his grandfather's statue in the cemetery
visages faces
Do cream and mantle become still and covered over
Oracle someone of infinite wisdom

Enter BASSANIO, LORENZO, *and* GRATIANO

Here comes Bassanio, your most noble kinsman,
Gratiano, and Lorenzo. Fare ye well;
We leave you now with better company.

SALARINO I would have stayed till I had made you merry, 60
If worthier friends had not prevented me.

ANTONIO Your worth is very dear in my regard.
I take it your own business calls on you,
And you embrace th'occasion to depart.

SALARINO Good morrow, my good lords. 65

BASSANIO Good signors both, when shall we laugh? Say, when?
You grow exceeding strange; must it be so?

SALARINO We'll make our leisures to attend on yours.
Exeunt Salarino and Solanio

LORENZO My Lord Bassanio, since you have found Antonio
We two will leave you, but at dinner time 70
I pray you have in mind where we must meet.

BASSANIO I will not fail you.

GRATIANO You look not well, Signor Antonio.
You have too much respect upon the world:
They lose it that do buy it with much care. 75
Believe me, you are marvellously changed.

ANTONIO I hold the world but as the world, Gratiano:
A stage where every man must play a part,
And mine a sad one.

GRATIANO Let me play the Fool.
With mirth and laughter let old wrinkles come, 80
And let my liver rather heat with wine
Than my heart cool with mortifying groans.
Why should a man whose blood is warm within
Sit like his grandsire cut in alabaster?
Sleep when he wakes? And creep into the jaundice 85
By being peevish? I tell thee what, Antonio –
I love thee, and it is my love that speaks –
There are a sort of men whose visages
Do cream and mantle like a standing pond,
And do a wilful stillness entertain, 90
With purpose to be dressed in an opinion
Of wisdom, gravity, profound conceit,
As who should say, 'I am Sir Oracle,
And when I ope my lips, let no dog bark!'

Gratiano advises Antonio against using sadness to gain a reputation for wisdom. Antonio asks Bassanio whom he loves. Bassanio begins by explaining his plans to pay off his debts.

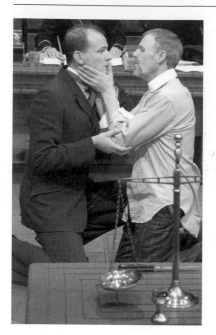

The relationship between Bassanio (left) and Antonio has become a much-discussed feature of productions of the play. Many have presented it as homoerotic: that Antonio is strongly attracted to Bassanio and, as he speaks, he often attempts to establish physical contact. Keep this notion in mind as you work through the play.

1 Money – a clue to character? (in small groups)

Bassanio has been asked about love, but he begins his answer by talking about his debts. He has spent all his money and owes a great deal.

One person reads aloud lines 121–33. The others echo every word to do with money. Afterwards, talk together about what the 'echoing' activity and the lines suggest about Bassanio's personality.

That therefore . . . nothing whose silence gains them a reputation for wisdom
this . . . opinion this stupid fish called reputation
exhortation strongly offered advice
gear advice (or business)
neat's tongue ox tongue
vendible desirable
secret pilgrimage journey of love

By something . . . grant continuance by enjoying a standard of living I could not afford
Nor . . . rate I don't complain about having to economise
prodigal wasteful
gaged owing
And . . . purposes because of our friendship I owe you an explanation

O my Antonio, I do know of these   95
That therefore only are reputed wise
For saying nothing; when I am very sure
If they should speak, would almost damn those ears
Which, hearing them, would call their brothers fools.
I'll tell thee more of this another time.   100
But fish not with this melancholy bait
For this fool gudgeon, this opinion.
Come, good Lorenzo. Fare ye well awhile;
I'll end my exhortation after dinner.

LORENZO Well, we will leave you then till dinner time.   105
I must be one of these same dumb wise men,
For Gratiano never lets me speak.

GRATIANO Well, keep me company but two years moe,
Thou shalt not know the sound of thine own tongue.

ANTONIO Farewell; I'll grow a talker for this gear.   110

GRATIANO Thanks, i'faith, for silence is only commendable
In a neat's tongue dried, and a maid not vendible.

Exeunt [Gratiano and Lorenzo]

ANTONIO It is that anything now.

BASSANIO Gratiano speaks an infinite deal of nothing, more than any
man in all Venice. His reasons are as two grains of wheat hid in two   115
bushels of chaff: you shall seek all day ere you find them, and when
you have them they are not worth the search.

ANTONIO Well, tell me now what lady is the same
To whom you swore a secret pilgrimage
That you today promised to tell me of.   120

BASSANIO 'Tis not unknown to you, Antonio,
How much I have disabled mine estate
By something showing a more swelling port
Than my faint means would grant continuance.
Nor do I now make moan to be abridged   125
From such a noble rate, but my chief care
Is to come fairly off from the great debts
Wherein my time, something too prodigal,
Hath left me gaged. To you, Antonio,
I owe the most in money and in love,   130
And from your love I have a warranty
To unburden all my plots and purposes
How to get clear of all the debts I owe.

Antonio is ready to help Bassanio, whatever the circumstances. Bassanio explains that he wishes to marry Portia, a wealthy heiress. Rich and famous men from all over the world come to woo her.

1 Antonio's pledge: 'My purse . . .' (in pairs)

In lines 134–8, Antonio offers everything to help his friend Bassanio. Take turns in reading the lines aloud, then talk together about Antonio's attitude towards Bassanio. Also discuss whether you think he is throwing good money after bad.

2 First impressions of Portia (in small groups)

In lines 160–71 the audience first hears of Portia. Bassanio uses stories of Ancient Greece and Rome to praise her. He compares her (line 165) to Portia who was the daughter of Cato, a famous Roman politician, and the wife of Brutus, the 'honourable man' who was one of Julius Caesar's assassins. Bassanio also sees her as a rich prize, like the Golden Fleece the Greek hero Jason sought in Colchis (see p. 181). These references would have been understood by educated members of Shakespeare's audience. They also indicate Bassanio's high social status.

a Read aloud lines 160–71. Each person reads up to a punctuation mark, then hands on. Emphasise all the words and phrases Bassanio uses to praise Portia.

b Write a paragraph giving your own impressions of Portia from Bassanio's description.

c Talk together about what Bassanio's classical references add to his description of Portia.

d Suggest at least two possible reasons why Shakespeare chose to have Bassanio begin the description of Portia by explaining that she is 'a lady richly left'.

And if . . . honour and if it's honourable, as you are
My purse . . . occasions everything I have is at your disposal
a wilful . . . lost like a stupid boy, I've lost every penny I've borrowed from you

To wind . . . circumstance to make use of my love for you in a roundabout way
prest unto forced into
a lady richly left a rich heiress

ANTONIO I pray you, good Bassanio, let me know it,
       And if it stand as you yourself still do   135
       Within the eye of honour, be assured
       My purse, my person, my extremest means
       Lie all unlocked to your occasions.

BASSANIO In my schooldays, when I had lost one shaft,
       I shot his fellow of the selfsame flight   140
       The selfsame way, with more advisèd watch
       To find the other forth; and by adventuring both
       I oft found both. I urge this childhood proof
       Because what follows is pure innocence.
       I owe you much, and like a wilful youth   145
       That which I owe is lost; but if you please
       To shoot another arrow that self way
       Which you did shoot the first, I do not doubt,
       As I will watch the aim, or to find both
       Or bring your latter hazard back again   150
       And thankfully rest debtor for the first.

ANTONIO You know me well, and herein spend but time
       To wind about my love with circumstance;
       And out of doubt you do me now more wrong
       In making question of my uttermost   155
       Than if you had made waste of all I have.
       Then do but say to me what I should do
       That in your knowledge may by me be done,
       And I am prest unto it: therefore speak.

BASSANIO In Belmont is a lady richly left,   160
       And she is fair, and – fairer than that word –
       Of wondrous virtues. Sometimes from her eyes
       I did receive fair speechless messages.
       Her name is Portia, nothing undervalued
       To Cato's daughter, Brutus' Portia.   165
       Nor is the wide world ignorant of her worth;
       For the four winds blow in from every coast
       Renownèd suitors, and her sunny locks
       Hang on her temples like a golden fleece,
       Which makes her seat of Belmont Colchos' strand,   170
       And many Jasons come in quest of her.

Antonio's cash is tied up in his ships, but he allows Bassanio to borrow money on his behalf. In Belmont, Portia complains that her dead father's will prevents her from choosing her own husband.

1 Bassanio's quest for credit (in small groups)

Antonio willingly agrees to finance Bassanio's journey to Belmont to woo Portia but his money is tied up in his trading ventures. Bassanio must use Antonio's reputation to secure credit. Take parts and improvise a meeting between Bassanio and his potential creditors.

2 Portia's weariness – like Antonio's sadness?

Portia's opening words echo Antonio's at the start of Scene 1. Look out in this scene for the reasons behind Portia's comment that she is 'aweary of this great world'. Compare them with your findings about Antonio's sadness in the first scene.

3 Nerissa's wisdom: in sixty seconds (in small groups)

Nerissa tells Portia that riches don't bring happiness:

> they are as sick that surfeit with too much as they that starve with nothing.

Talk together about whether you think this might be Shakespeare's comment on the characters appearing in Scene 1. Then use Nerissa's words as the title for your own sixty-second theatre. Your play should be no longer than a minute, and must show Nerissa's words in action.

I . . . thrift I feel I'm going to make a huge profit

at sea invested in my ships

racked . . . to the uttermost stretched to the limit

presently immediately

To have . . . sake on my credit or for the sake of friendship

surfeit overfeed

seated in the mean of average wealth

superfluity . . . longer too much good living ages us; having just enough makes us live longer

divine priest

The brain . . . decree the head is overruled by the heart

meshes nets

But . . . husband all this talking won't help me find a man

O my Antonio, had I but the means
To hold a rival place with one of them,
I have a mind presages me such thrift
That I should questionless be fortunate.   175

ANTONIO Thou know'st that all my fortunes are at sea;
Neither have I money nor commodity
To raise a present sum; therefore go forth,
Try what my credit can in Venice do,
That shall be racked even to the uttermost   180
To furnish thee to Belmont to fair Portia.
Go presently enquire, and so will I,
Where money is, and I no question make
To have it of my trust or for my sake.

Exeunt

Act 1 Scene 2
Belmont   The garden of Portia's house

Enter PORTIA and NERISSA

PORTIA By my troth, Nerissa, my little body is aweary of this great
world.

NERISSA You would be, sweet madam, if your miseries were in the
same abundance as your good fortunes are; and yet for aught I see,
they are as sick that surfeit with too much as they that starve with   5
nothing. It is no mean happiness, therefore, to be seated in the
mean - superfluity comes sooner by white hairs, but competency
lives longer.

PORTIA Good sentences, and well pronounced.

NERISSA They would be better if well followed.   10

PORTIA If to do were as easy as to know what were good to do, chapels
had been churches, and poor men's cottages princes' palaces. It is
a good divine that follows his own instructions; I can easier teach
twenty what were good to be done, than be one of the twenty to
follow mine own teaching. The brain may devise laws for the   15
blood, but a hot temper leaps o'er a cold decree – such a hare is
madness the youth, to skip o'er the meshes of good counsel the
cripple. But this reasoning is not in the fashion to choose me a
husband. O me, the word 'choose'! I may neither choose who I
would, nor refuse who I dislike, so is the will of a living daughter   20
curbed by the will of a dead father. Is it not hard, Nerissa, that I
cannot choose one, nor refuse none?

Nerissa recaps the will: potential husbands (suitors) must choose between three caskets of gold, silver and lead. Whoever chooses correctly wins Portia! Nerissa begins describing Portia's suitors.

1 Belmont: a patriarchal world?

Although she is mistress of Belmont's immense wealth, Portia's freedom is strictly limited by the conditions of her dead father's will. It seems that she will be given a husband in an extreme form of an arranged marriage: 'so is the will of a living daughter curbed by the will of a dead father'. When you turn the page you will find an activity on the men who have come to Belmont in the hope of marrying Portia.

a **Portia's father**   The audience is not told much about the former master of Belmont. What can you deduce about him from lines 19–29? Write a pen portrait of Portia's father.

b **The will**   Portia's father has left a will, setting out the conditions for her marriage. Make up a copy of the will, ensuring you include the terms described in lines 23–7. Try to use the language of a legal document.

c **Arranged marriages**   Marriages in which partners are chosen by the parents are a feature of some modern societies. Make lists of the advantages and disadvantages of arranged marriages.

d **What do you think?**   Work in small groups. Talk together about Portia's predicament, and explore how far some young women today might face similar restrictions on their freedom to choose a husband.

---

his meaning   the one he intended
over-name   list
level at   guess
colt   rough young man
and he makes it . . . himself   he is proud of being able to shoe his own horse

played false   had sex
he is . . . man   he copies everyone, but has no personality of his own
throstle   thrush
he falls . . . a-capering   he starts dancing about
requite him   love him in return

NERISSA Your father was ever virtuous; and holy men at their death have good inspirations. Therefore the lottery that he hath devised in these three chests of gold, silver, and lead, whereof who chooses his meaning chooses you, will no doubt never be chosen by any rightly but one who you shall rightly love. But what warmth is there in your affection towards any of these princely suitors that are already come? 25

PORTIA I pray thee over-name them, and as thou namest them I will describe them – and according to my description, level at my affection. 30

NERISSA First, there is the Neapolitan prince.

PORTIA Ay, that's a colt indeed, for he doth nothing but talk of his horse; and he makes it a great appropriation to his own good parts that he can shoe him himself. I am much afeared my lady his mother played false with a smith. 35

NERISSA Then is there the County Palatine.

PORTIA He doth nothing but frown, as who should say, 'And you will not have me, choose.' He hears merry tales and smiles not; I fear he will prove the weeping philosopher when he grows old, being so full of unmannerly sadness in his youth. I had rather be married to a death's head with a bone in his mouth than to either of these. God defend me from these two! 40

NERISSA How say you by the French lord, Monsieur Le Bon? 45

PORTIA God made him, and therefore let him pass for a man. In truth I know it is a sin to be a mocker, but he! – why, he hath a horse better than the Neapolitan's, a better bad habit of frowning than the Count Palatine: he is every man in no man. If a throstle sing, he falls straight a-capering; he will fence with his own shadow. If I should marry him, I should marry twenty husbands. If he would despise me, I would forgive him; for if he love me to madness, I shall never requite him. 50

NERISSA What say you then to Falconbridge, the young baron of England? 55

The two women end their mocking of Portia's suitors. Nerissa reports the men's intention to return home immediately. She reminds Portia of her past meeting with Bassanio.

1 Six suitors: a mini-pageant (in groups of six)

Lines 30–81 describe Portia's six suitors:

The Neapolitan prince (lines 33–7) is a 'colt', obsessed with horses.
The County Palatine (lines 38–44) is too sad and melancholy.
The Frenchman (lines 45–53) merely copies people and has no personality: 'he is every man in no man'.
The Englishman (lines 54–62) is uneducated, and dresses and behaves badly.
The Scotsman (lines 63–7) is a brawler.
The German (lines 68–81) is a drunkard.

Each person steps into role as a different suitor:

- Devise a suitable coat of arms and motto for your character.
- Experiment with ways of portraying your suitor, according to Portia's description.
- Present your work to the rest of the class in mini-pageant form: the grand entry of your suitors to Belmont.

2 National stereotypes (in pairs)

In Shakespeare's time the suitors were recognised as national stereotypes and Portia's descriptions probably evoked laughter from the audience. But stereotyping is unfair and inaccurate and Portia's words contain a scornful and racist edge.

a Talk together about how Portia might be seen as intolerant and dismissive of those outside her own society.

b Identify at least two examples of national stereotyping in films and television programmes.

---

dumbshow   a mimed play
borrowed . . . ear   was punched on the ear
became his surety . . . another   was also struck by the Englishman and swore to pay him back

determinations   plans
Sibylla   Greek prophetess (she could live as many years as she could hold grains of sand)
Diana   goddess of chastity (virginity) and the moon

PORTIA You know I say nothing to him, for he understands not me, nor I him: he hath neither Latin, French, nor Italian, and you will come into the court and swear that I have a poor penny-worth in the English. He is a proper man's picture, but alas who can converse with a dumbshow? How oddly he is suited! I think he bought his 60 doublet in Italy, his round hose in France, his bonnet in Germany, and his behaviour everywhere.

NERISSA What think you of the Scottish lord his neighbour?

PORTIA That he hath a neighbourly charity in him, for he borrowed a box of the ear of the Englishman and swore he would pay him again 65 when he was able. I think the Frenchman became his surety and sealed under for another.

NERISSA How like you the young German, the Duke of Saxony's nephew?

PORTIA Very vilely in the morning when he is sober, and most vilely 70 in the afternoon when he is drunk. When he is best he is a little worse than a man, and when he is worst he is little better than a beast. And the worst fall that ever fell, I hope I shall make shift to go without him.

NERISSA If he should offer to choose, and choose the right casket, you 75 should refuse to perform your father's will if you should refuse to accept him.

PORTIA Therefore, for fear of the worst, I pray thee set a deep glass of Rhenish wine on the contrary casket, for if the devil be within, and that temptation without, I know he will choose it. I will do any- 80 thing, Nerissa, ere I will be married to a sponge.

NERISSA You need not fear, lady, the having any of these lords. They have acquainted me with their determinations, which is indeed to return to their home, and to trouble you with no more suit unless you may be won by some other sort than your father's imposition, 85 depending on the caskets.

PORTIA If I live to be as old as Sibylla, I will die as chaste as Diana unless I be obtained by the manner of my father's will. I am glad this parcel of wooers are so reasonable, for there is not one among them but I dote on his very absence; and I pray God grant them 90 a fair departure.

NERISSA Do you not remember, lady, in your father's time, a Venetian, a scholar and a soldier, that came hither in company of the Marquis of Montferrat?

A servant announces that the suitors are about to leave, and that another, the Prince of Morocco, will soon arrive. In Venice, Bassanio tries to borrow money from Shylock.

1 Hints of love – and hate? (in pairs)

a Love?   In performance, most actors playing Portia use the few words she speaks about Bassanio to show that she is already deeply attracted to him, but tries not to show it. Take turns to speak lines 95 and 98–9 in ways to bring out that impression. Afterwards, talk together about whether you think this makes Portia more interesting to the audience and is dramatically effective.

b Hate?   Speak lines 105–8 and then talk together about what they suggest to you about Portia. Your response to Activity 2 on page 16 is relevant here.

2 First read-through (in groups of three)

Scene 3 introduces Shylock. The best thing to do first is to take parts as Shylock, Bassanio and Antonio and speak the whole scene. Don't pause over anything you don't understand. Just read through to gain a first impression of Shylock and the 'bond'. Afterwards, work on some of the activities provided.

3 Shylock: repetitions (in pairs)

Shylock's first words are about money. Take parts and read lines 1–12. Notice that words are repeated and echoed ('three', 'well', 'bound'). Experiment with different ways of sparring verbally in these lines. Sometimes the lines are played in a 'cat and mouse' fashion as Shylock keeps testing Bassanio's patience. Who do you think controls this exchange?

---

forerunner   messenger
condition   character
complexion . . . devil   Elizabethans
  believed that devils were black
I had . . . wive me   I would rather he
  be my priest than my husband

sirrah   my man
ducats   gold coins, coins of the duke
shall be bound   will have to repay
Have . . . contrary?   Have you heard
  differently?

PORTIA Yes, yes, it was Bassanio! – as I think so was he called. 95

NERISSA True, madam; he of all the men that ever my foolish eyes looked upon was the best deserving a fair lady.

PORTIA I remember him well, and I remember him worthy of thy praise.

Enter a SERVINGMAN

How now, what news? 100

SERVINGMAN The four strangers seek for you, madam, to take their leave; and there is a forerunner come from a fifth, the Prince of Morocco, who brings word the prince his master will be here tonight.

PORTIA If I could bid the fifth welcome with so good heart as I can bid 105
the other four farewell, I should be glad of his approach. If he have the condition of a saint, and the complexion of a devil, I had rather he should shrive me than wive me.

Come, Nerissa; sirrah, go before:
Whiles we shut the gate upon one wooer, another knocks at 110
the door

Exeunt

Act 1 Scene 3
Venice

Enter BASSANIO *with* SHYLOCK *the Jew*

SHYLOCK Three thousand ducats, well.

BASSANIO Ay, sir, for three months.

SHYLOCK For three months, well.

BASSANIO For the which, as I told you, Antonio shall be bound.

SHYLOCK Antonio shall become bound, well. 5

BASSANIO May you stead me? Will you pleasure me? Shall I know your answer?

SHYLOCK Three thousand ducats for three months, and Antonio bound.

BASSANIO Your answer to that? 10

SHYLOCK Antonio is a good man –

BASSANIO Have you heard any imputation to the contrary?

Shylock doubts the security of Antonio's ships, but seems willing to lend the money. He tells the audience that he hates Antonio for a variety of reasons, and intends to harm him if he can.

1 Focus on Shylock (in pairs)

a **Making a joke**   Look carefully at lines 18–21. Shylock plays on the words 'rats' and 'pirates'. Is he making a joke of it? Take it in turns to read the lines aloud, first seriously, and then jokingly. How should Bassanio respond?

b **An invitation to dinner**   How should Shylock speak lines 27–31? On stage they are often performed as sincere and serious, but is he still being playful and joking with Bassanio? Talk about how you think they should be delivered.

c **Shylock's hatred of Antonio**   An Aside is a remark made by a character to the audience. By convention it is unheard by the other people on stage. One reads aloud Shylock's Aside in lines 33–44; the other echoes words which show Shylock's hatred for Antonio. Try this several times, then talk together about why Shylock hates Antonio so passionately.

2 Now it's Antonio's turn!

What if at this point Shakespeare had also written an Aside for Antonio to voice his feelings about Shylock? Try writing one yourself, but first look at lines 40–3, where Shylock describes Antonio's view of him and his race. The 2004 film of the play opened with a sequence in which Antonio was seen spitting on Shylock.

Try to write Antonio's Aside in the same style and rhythm as Shylock's (see p. 184).

---

good   financially sound
supposition   doubt
Rialto   Stock Exchange of Venice
squandered   scattered
bethink me   think carefully about this
to eat . . . devil into   to eat pig which Jesus conjured devils into from madmen's minds (see Matthew 8: 28–32)

publican   taxman
gratis   without charging interest
rate of usance   rate of interest
upon the hip   in a weak spot
rails   criticises
thrift   profit
I am . . . store   I'm working out how much ready cash I've got

SHYLOCK Ho no, no, no, no: my meaning in saying he is a good man is to have you understand me that he is sufficient. Yet his means are in supposition: he hath an argosy bound to Tripolis, another to the Indies; I understand moreover upon the Rialto he hath a third at Mexico, a fourth for England, and other ventures he hath squandered abroad. But ships are but boards, sailors but men; there be land rats, and water rats, water thieves and land thieves – I mean pirates – and then there is the peril of waters, winds and rocks. The man is notwithstanding sufficient. Three thousand ducats: I think I may take his bond. 15

20

BASSANIO Be assured you may.

SHYLOCK I will be assured I may; and that I may be assured, I will bethink me – may I speak with Antonio? 25

BASSANIO If it please you to dine with us –

SHYLOCK Yes, to smell pork, to eat of the habitation which your prophet the Nazarite conjured the devil into. I will buy with you, sell with you, talk with you, walk with you, and so following; but I will not eat with you, drink with you, nor pray with you. What news on the Rialto? Who is he comes here? 30

Enter ANTONIO

BASSANIO This is Signor Antonio.

SHYLOCK [*Aside*] How like a fawning publican he looks!
      I hate him for he is a Christian;
      But more, for that in low simplicity 35
      He lends out money gratis, and brings down
      The rate of usance here with us in Venice.
      If I can catch him once upon the hip,
      I will feed fat the ancient grudge I bear him.
      He hates our sacred nation, and he rails 40
      Even there where merchants most do congregate
      On me, my bargains, and my well-won thrift
      Which he calls interest. Cursed be my tribe
      If I forgive him!

BASSANIO   Shylock, do you hear?

SHYLOCK I am debating of my present store, 45
      And by the near guess of my memory
      I cannot instantly raise up the gross
      Of full three thousand ducats. What of that?

Shylock gently taunts Antonio for his past opposition to charging interest. He tells a story from the Bible to show the benefits of profiting by lending.

1 Veiled contempt? (in pairs)

This is the first exchange between Antonio and Shylock in the play (see picture at top of p. v). Actors like to use these lines to show how the relationship is strained, with enmity and loathing barely under control on both sides. Antonio dislikes both Jews and money-lending, but he has to ask Shylock for a loan. Choose parts and read aloud lines 56–62. Pause after each sentence to voice the secret thoughts of your character. (This is like speaking the thought bubbles in a comic strip.)

2 Jacob and his sheep

Shylock uses a Bible story (Book of Genesis chapter 30) to justify his way of doing business. Jacob, a descendant of Abraham, agreed to look after his Uncle Laban's sheep. In return he could keep any new-born lambs which were streaked or multicoloured. During the mating season he made a fence of branches ('wands') partly stripped ('pilled') of their bark, so that the ewes would see the fence when they conceived (it was believed that offspring resemble what the mother sees at conception). As a result of Jacob's ingenuity, a large number of streaked lambs were born, which he could keep for himself.

a Shylock's insistence that 'thrift is blessing' makes a clear connection between religion and profit. Shylock's story can be difficult to follow, but speak it like a developing logical argument ending in a very emphatic conclusion in lines 81–2.

b Make a tableau to show Bassanio's and Antonio's reaction to Shylock's long tale (Antonio's verbal response is on the next page).

---

in our mouths we mentioned (Does it also refer to Shylock's verbal savaging of Antonio?)
I neither ... excess I don't lend or borrow for profit
ripe wants urgent needs
Is he ... would? Does he know how much you want?

compromised agreed
eanlings new-born lambs
hire wages
rank ready to mate
work of generation mating
And in ... kind during mating
fulsome ewes randy sheep

Tubal, a wealthy Hebrew of my tribe,
Will furnish me. But soft, how many months   50
Do you desire? [*To Antonio*] Rest you fair, good signor!
Your worship was the last man in our mouths.
ANTONIO Shylock, albeit I neither lend nor borrow
By taking nor by giving of excess,
Yet to supply the ripe wants of my friend   55
I'll break a custom. [*To Bassanio*] Is he yet possessed
How much ye would?
SHYLOCK   Ay, ay, three thousand ducats.
ANTONIO And for three months.
SHYLOCK I had forgot, three months; [*To Bassanio*] you told me so.
Well then, your bond; and let me see – but hear you,   60
Methoughts you said you neither lend nor borrow
Upon advantage.
ANTONIO   I do never use it.
SHYLOCK When Jacob grazed his uncle Laban's sheep –
This Jacob from our holy Abram was
(As his wise mother wrought in his behalf)   65
The third possessor; ay, he was the third –
ANTONIO And what of him, did he take interest?
SHYLOCK No, not take interest, not as you would say
Directly interest. Mark what Jacob did:
When Laban and himself were compromised   70
That all the eanlings which were streaked and pied
Should fall as Jacob's hire, the ewes being rank
In end of autumn turnèd to the rams,
And when the work of generation was
Between these woolly breeders in the act,   75
The skilful shepherd pilled me certain wands
And in the doing of the deed of kind
He stuck them up before the fulsome ewes,
Who then conceiving, did in eaning time
Fall parti-coloured lambs, and those were Jacob's.   80
This was a way to thrive, and he was blest;
And thrift is blessing if men steal it not.

Antonio is not convinced by Shylock's argument. He warns Bassanio not to be deceived by the Jew's use of the Bible. Shylock reminds Antonio of the contemptuous way he has been treated in the past.

1 Expressions of scorn

Antonio contemptuously dismisses Shylock's parable, ignores Shylock's joke in line 88, and interrupts him to warn Bassanio against Bible-quoting villains.

a In some productions, Shylock overhears Antonio's lines 89–94. In others he does not. Which of these stagings do you think would have the greatest dramatic effect? Why?

b Is 'The devil' meant to be Shylock, or Lucifer himself?

c Shakespeare often used the image of the smiling villain, for example in *Macbeth*, *Hamlet* and *Richard III*. Suggest why Antonio calls Shylock 'a villain with a smiling cheek'.

2 Shylock versus Antonio (in pairs)

a Take turns to speak and perform Shylock's lines 98–121 to each other. Experiment with different tones of voice, gestures and the positioning of the two enemies. Emphasise key words and phrases. In one production, Shylock stood face to face with Antonio. In another, Shylock lay relaxed on cushions and spoke in a half-amused tone. In yet another, Shylock sneered at and mocked Antonio as he circled him, whining in mockery of his reply. Work out what you think is the most appropriate staging.

b Make a list of Shylock's grievances against Antonio.

c Select what you think is the image or line that most tellingly captures Shylock's anger against his Christian tormentors. Say why you think it is so revealing.

This was . . . heaven God was responsible for Jacob's good luck
inserted mentioned
holy witness evidence from the Bible
beholding indebted
rated insulted
gaberdine coat
void your rheum spit
stranger cur stray dog
bondman's key slave's voice

ANTONIO This was a venture, sir, that Jacob served for,
A thing not in his power to bring to pass,
But swayed and fashioned by the hand of heaven. 85
Was this inserted to make interest good?
Or is your gold and silver ewes and rams?
SHYLOCK I cannot tell, I make it breed as fast.
But note me, signor –
ANTONIO   Mark you this, Bassanio,
The devil can cite Scripture for his purpose. 90
An evil soul producing holy witness
Is like a villain with a smiling cheek,
A goodly apple rotten at the heart.
O what a goodly outside falsehood hath!
SHYLOCK Three thousand ducats, 'tis a good round sum. 95
Three months from twelve, then let me see, the rate –
ANTONIO Well, Shylock, shall we be beholding to you?
SHYLOCK Signor Antonio, many a time and oft
In the Rialto you have rated me
About my monies and my usances. 100
Still have I borne it with a patient shrug
For suff'rance is the badge of all our tribe.
You call me misbeliever, cut-throat dog,
And spit upon my Jewish gaberdine,
And all for use of that which is mine own. 105
Well then, it now appears you need my help.
Go to, then, you come to me, and you say,
'Shylock, we would have monies' – you say so,
You that did void your rheum upon my beard,
And foot me as you spurn a stranger cur 110
Over your threshold: monies is your suit.
What should I say to you? Should I not say
'Hath a dog money? Is it possible
A cur can lend three thousand ducats?' Or
Shall I bend low, and in a bondman's key, 115
With bated breath and whisp'ring humbleness,
Say this:
'Fair sir, you spat on me on Wednesday last,
You spurned me such a day, another time
You called me dog: and for these courtesies 120
I'll lend you thus much monies.'

Antonio remains contemptuous, but Shylock claims to want his friendship, offering not to charge interest on the loan. Instead, if Antonio fails to pay, Shylock will take a pound of his flesh.

1 Shylock backs down (in pairs)

Take parts and read lines 122–35. Imagine you are directing the play. Write notes for the actors about how they could speak these lines to achieve greatest dramatic effect. How angry (if at all) should Antonio be? Why does Shylock seem to back down and claim he wishes friendship and love?

2 Friends don't profit from each other

Antonio's reply to Shylock's taunting (lines 122–9) reveals his deep prejudice against Shylock and his money-lending ways. Friends should not take advantage of each other by charging interest ('A breed for barren metal') and making money from money. Talk together about what you think are the rights and wrongs of charging interest.

3 The 'single bond' – 'a merry sport'?

Shylock proposes 'a merry sport': if Antonio cannot repay the loan, he must forfeit a pound of his flesh.

a Imagine you are the notary. Write your own version of the bond between Shylock and Antonio. This bond is a formal business document, so use appropriate language. Include all the agreed terms of the loan, and add the signatures of both parties and witnesses.

b There has been argument for centuries about whether or not Shylock thinks up 'the pound of flesh' on the spur of the moment, or whether he had it in mind earlier. What do you think? There is also argument over whether, at this moment, he intends it seriously or just as 'a merry sport'. Join in the debate! But first try different ways of speaking lines 136–44 to test out these various views – which interpretation of the lines seems most plausible and effective to you?

---

take . . . friend   make money from lending to a friend
break   goes bankrupt
no doit / Of usance   not one penny of interest

notary   lawyer
in a merry sport   just for a joke
I'll . . . necessity   I'd rather stay in debt
exaction . . . forfeiture   demanding the forfeit (the pound of flesh)

ANTONIO I am as like to call thee so again,
        To spit on thee again, to spurn thee too.
        If thou wilt lend this money, lend it not
        As to thy friends, for when did friendship take   125
        A breed for barren metal of his friend?
        But lend it rather to thine enemy,
        Who if he break, thou mayst with better face
        Exact the penalty.
SHYLOCK Why look you how you storm!   130
        I would be friends with you, and have your love,
        Forget the shames that you have stained me with,
        Supply your present wants, and take no doit
        Of usance for my monies, and you'll not hear me.
        This is kind I offer.
BASSANIO   This were kindness.   135
SHYLOCK This kindness will I show.
        Go with me to a notary, seal me there
        Your single bond, and, in a merry sport,
        If you repay me not on such a day,
        In such a place, such sum or sums as are   140
        Expressed in the condition, let the forfeit
        Be nominated for an equal pound
        Of your fair flesh, to be cut off and taken
        In what part of your body pleaseth me.
ANTONIO Content, in faith! I'll seal to such a bond,   145
        And say there is much kindness in the Jew.
BASSANIO You shall not seal to such a bond for me;
        I'll rather dwell in my necessity.
ANTONIO Why, fear not, man, I will not forfeit it.
        Within these two months, that's a month before   150
        This bond expires, I do expect return
        Of thrice three times the value of this bond.
SHYLOCK O father Abram, what these Christians are,
        Whose own hard dealings teaches them suspect
        The thoughts of others! Pray you tell me this: 155
        If he should break his day what should I gain
        By the exaction of the forfeiture?

Shylock insists that he can gain nothing from the deal except Antonio's friendship. Antonio agrees to the terms, and Shylock leaves to fetch the money. Bassanio is still uneasy about the contract.

1 'A pound of man's flesh' – 'this friendship' (in pairs)

Activity 3 on page 26 invited your views on whether Shylock is serious or not in proposing the pound of flesh as bond. Shylock now makes light of the forfeit and again describes the bond as 'merry'. What non-verbal actions would you give to Shylock to accompany his lines 158–62?

2 A rhyming couplet for Shylock

The last four lines (171–4) are rhyming couplets (they rhyme in pairs). Write your own rhyming couplet as two exit lines for Shylock in which he comments on the bond.

Look closely at this 1932 set design for the Rialto. It can be either the Stock Exchange or a bridge, depending on the director's intentions. Talk about what this set suggests about life in Venice. How does it fit in with the ideas you have so far developed about the city as presented in the play?

---

muttons, beefs sheep and cattle
adieu goodbye

unthrifty knave careless servant
presently immediately

A pound of man's flesh, taken from a man,
Is not so estimable, profitable neither,
As flesh of muttons, beefs, or goats. I say   160
To buy his favour, I extend this friendship.
If he will take it, so; if not, adieu,
And for my love, I pray you wrong me not.
ANTONIO Yes, Shylock, I will seal unto this bond.
SHYLOCK Then meet me forthwith at the notary's.   165
Give him direction for this merry bond,
And I will go and purse the ducats straight,
See to my house left in the fearful guard
Of an unthrifty knave, and presently
I'll be with you.   *Exit*
ANTONIO   Hie thee, gentle Jew.   170
The Hebrew will turn Christian, he grows kind.
BASSANIO I like not fair terms and a villain's mind.
ANTONIO Come on, in this there can be no dismay,
My ships come home a month before the day.
                                        Exeunt

Looking back at Act 1
Activities for groups or individuals

1 Venice and Belmont: a world of commerce and a world of dreams

Act 1 establishes two seemingly different worlds. Venice is portrayed as a patriarchal world of money and commerce. In contrast, Belmont seems a feminine world of romance, trading in love. Write down your impressions of what life is like in Shylock's Venice and Portia's Belmont. Think about such matters as religion, class, occupations, attitudes to race, and the roles of men and women. Use your ideas to design two stage settings to show the difference between the two worlds of the play.

2 Conflict

Act 1 portrays all kinds of conflicts, some evident for all to see, and some hidden below the surface. The clearest sign of conflict to come is the ominous bond that Shylock describes as 'a merry sport'. Make a list of all the conflicts you can detect in Act 1. You will find more to add to your list as you read on.

3 Antonio: a case study

What do you make of Antonio? He is obviously popular with his friends and has a close relationship with Bassanio, but he has been cruel to Shylock. He is also depressed, though there is no clear explanation for his sadness. Imagine you are a psychiatrist. Write a case study of Antonio based on his language, his behaviour, and what others have said about him in Act 1.

4 Continuing conversations

At the start of all three scenes in Act 1 the characters enter already deep in conversation. Choose one scene and script the characters' conversation before the scene begins.

5 Shylock's Asides

No one knows for certain which lines Shakespeare intended to be spoken directly to the audience as Asides. Over the centuries, editors of the plays have made their own judgements about which lines are

Asides and which are not, and in every production, actors have done the same. Imagine you are playing Shylock. Look through Scene 3 and decide which of his lines you would speak as Asides. Give reasons for your choices.

6 Agreeing the bond

a What line from Act 1 Scene 3 do you think Antonio is speaking in the picture below?

b Bassanio warns Antonio about the bond: 'I like not fair terms and a villain's mind.' Imagine that you are Antonio. Write a few paragraphs about what you think of Shylock's 'bond'. Is Shylock showing genuine friendship or do you feel that he has sinister intentions in mind as he proposes his 'merry sport'?

The prince of Morocco arrives to try to win Portia's hand in marriage. Portia stresses that she must obey her dead father's will and marry the man who solves the riddle of the caskets.

1 A grand entry (in large groups)

Morocco has come to Belmont to seek Portia's hand in marriage. He wants to create an impression of his eminence and importance. Study the stage direction at the beginning of the scene, then act out the entrance of the two groups of characters. Highlight the sense of ceremony. You could add appropriate music.

2 Morocco readies himself (in pairs)

This is a short scene preparing for Morocco's choice. Every production has to decide just how to present Morocco and Portia. Read the whole scene first, then choose from the following activities.

a **Morocco: serious, or comic, or . . .?** Is Morocco noble and dignified, a comic windbag, or . . .? Take it in turns to read aloud Morocco's two speeches (lines 1–12 and lines 22–38). Using voice and gesture:

- make them exaggerated and funny
- make them sensational and melodramatic
- read them as seriously as you can, to show him as genuinely noble.

Morocco is described in the stage direction as a 'tawny Moor'. He asks Portia not to dislike him for the colour of his skin (lines 1–2). Talk together about why Shakespeare chooses to include these sensitive details.

b **Portia: a study in sincerity?** Take turns to speak Portia's lines 13–22. Although she is being polite to Morocco, what do you think she really feels about the possibility of being married to him? She also seems critical of her dead father, referring to the way in which he 'scanted' (restricted) and 'hedged' (limited) her actions. Try reading the speech again to bring out the tension between her duty to her dead father's will and her feelings towards Morocco.

---

shadowed livery	dark uniform	**scanted**	restricted
burnished	brightly polished	**hedged**	limited
Phoebus	the sun god	**scimitar**	sword with a curved blade
feared	terrified	**Sophy**	Shah of Persia
clime	climate	**fields**	battles
nice	over-fussy	**a roars**	he roars

Act 2 Scene 1
Belmont   A room in Portia's house

A flourish of cornets. Enter the Prince of MOROCCO, a tawny Moor all in white, and three or four followers accordingly; with PORTIA, NERISSA, and their train

MOROCCO Mislike me not for my complexion,
        The shadowed livery of the burnished sun,
        To whom I am a neighbour and near bred.
        Bring me the fairest creature northward born,
        Where Phoebus' fire scarce thaws the icicles,   5
        And let us make incision for your love
        To prove whose blood is reddest, his or mine.
        I tell thee, lady, this aspèct of mine
        Hath feared the valiant; by my love I swear
        The best-regarded virgins of our clime   10
        Have loved it too. I would not change this hue,
        Except to steal your thoughts, my gentle queen.
PORTIA In terms of choice I am not solely led
        By nice direction of a maiden's eyes.
        Besides, the lottery of my destiny   15
        Bars me the right of voluntary choosing.
        But if my father had not scanted me,
        And hedged me by his wit to yield myself
        His wife who wins me by that means I told you,
        Yourself, renownèd prince, then stood as fair   20
        As any comer I have looked on yet
        For my affection.
MOROCCO   Even for that I thank you.
        Therefore I pray you lead me to the caskets
        To try my fortune. By this scimitar,
        That slew the Sophy and a Persian prince   25
        That won three fields of Sultan Solyman,
        I would o'er-stare the sternest eyes that look,
        Outbrave the heart most daring on the earth,
        Pluck the young sucking cubs from the she-bear,
        Yea, mock the lion when a roars for prey,   30

Portia reminds Morocco that he must swear an oath and, after dinner, is to make his choice of casket. Scene 2 introduces Lancelot Gobbo, Shylock's servant, who is considering deserting his master.

1 The audience's second look at Portia

This is the second scene to feature Portia: she appeared before in Act 1 Scene 2 describing her suitors to Nerissa. Compile a list of differences you can spot between her manner of speaking privately, to her lady-in-waiting, and publicly in this courtship ritual.

2 'Forward to the temple' – Morocco's thoughts

At 'the temple' (Belmont's church) Morocco must swear an oath never to marry if he chooses the wrong casket. The consequences of failure are high, yet success rests on a lottery. Write a short monologue for Morocco in which you capture the tension and anxiety of his predicament.

3 Lancelot v. 'conscience' v. 'fiend' (in groups of three)

Lines 1–24 of Scene 2 are a **soliloquy** (a speech delivered by one character alone on stage). Lancelot is debating whether to leave his master but he never uses Shylock's name, referring to him as 'the Jew' and confusing his words so that 'incarnate' comically becomes 'incarnation'.

Read aloud Lancelot's speech. One person plays Lancelot Gobbo, another speaks and acts as his 'conscience' and the third as 'the fiend'. Add actions and gestures to emphasise the debate that is taking place in Lancelot's mind.

In the light of this experience, what advice would you give to an actor about performing this speech? Do you think that the speech is meant to be contemptuous, humorous or . . .?

Hercules and Lichas a legendary Greek hero and his servant
Alcides another name for Hercules
hazard gamble

will serve me will permit me
fiend devil
pack be gone
did something smack was like that (or kissed noisily)

To win thee, lady. But alas the while,
If Hercules and Lichas play at dice
Which is the better man, the greater throw
May turn by fortune from the weaker hand.
So is Alcides beaten by his rage,   35
And so may I, blind Fortune leading me,
Miss that which one unworthier may attain,
And die with grieving.

PORTIA   You must take your chance,
And either not attempt to choose at all
Or swear before you choose, if you choose wrong,   40
Never to speak to lady afterward
In way of marriage: therefore be advised.

MOROCCO Nor will not. Come, bring me unto my chance.

PORTIA First forward to the temple; after dinner
Your hazard shall be made.

MOROCCO   Good fortune then,   45
To make me blest – or cursèd'st among men!

Cornets. Exeunt

Act 2 Scene 2
Venice   Near Shylock's house

Enter LANCELOT GOBBO, the Clown, alone

LANCELOT Certainly, my conscience will serve me to run from this Jew
my master. The fiend is at mine elbow and tempts me, saying to me
'Gobbo, Lancelot Gobbo, good Lancelot', or 'Good Gobbo', or
'Good Lancelot Gobbo, use your legs, take the start, run away.'
My conscience says 'No: take heed, honest Lancelot, take heed,   5
honest Gobbo' – or (as aforesaid) – 'honest Lancelot Gobbo; do
not run, scorn running with thy heels.' Well, the most courageous
fiend bids me pack. 'Fia!' says the fiend, 'Away!' says the fiend.
''Fore the heavens, rouse up a brave mind', says the fiend, 'and
run.' Well, my conscience, hanging about the neck of my heart,   10
says very wisely to me, 'My honest friend Lancelot, being an honest
man's son, or rather an honest woman's son' (for indeed my
father did something smack, something grow to; he had a kind of
taste): well, my conscience says 'Lancelot, budge not!' 'Budge!'

Lancelot Gobbo resolves to leave Shylock's service. Lancelot's nearly blind father arrives, looking for Lancelot, but does not recognise his son. Lancelot decides to play a trick on him.

1 Down and out in Venice?

Write a paragraph about how this picture contrasts with what you have so far seen of Venice and Belmont.

2 'I will try confusions with him' (in pairs)

Focus on the exchange between Lancelot and his father (lines 25–92). Sometimes audiences find it tedious or incomprehensible or distasteful.

a Take parts and read through, thinking about whether Lancelot uses his voice to deceive Gobbo, and whether you feel it is humorous or merely cruel.

b Improvise an argument between someone who likes this part of the scene and someone who disapproves of it as being in bad taste and irrelevant.

---

incarnation Lancelot means 'incarnate' ('made flesh')
sand-blind half-blind
gravel-blind nearly totally blind
Marry by St Mary

Be God's sonties by God's saints
raise the waters make him cry
a will he will
ergo therefore
the sisters three the three Fates who decide human destiny

says the fiend. 'Budge not!' says my conscience. 'Conscience', say   15
I, 'you counsel well.' 'Fiend', say I, 'you counsel well.' To be
ruled by my conscience, I should stay with the Jew my master
who – God bless the mark! – is a kind of devil; and to run away
from the Jew, I should be ruled by the fiend who – saving your
reverence – is the devil himself. Certainly the Jew is the very devil   20
incarnation, and, in my conscience, my conscience is but a kind of
hard conscience to offer to counsel me to stay with the Jew. The
fiend gives the more friendly counsel: I will run, fiend, my heels
are at your commandment, I will run.

Enter OLD GOBBO *with a basket*

GOBBO Master young-man, you, I pray you, which is the way to Master   25
  Jew's?
LANCELOT [*Aside*] O heavens! This is my true-begotten father who
  being more than sand-blind, high gravel-blind, knows me not. I
  will try confusions with him.
GOBBO Master young-gentleman, I pray you, which is the way to   30
  Master Jew's?
LANCELOT Turn upon your right hand at the next turning, but at the
  next turning of all on your left. Marry, at the very next turning
  turn of no hand but turn down indirectly to the Jew's house.
GOBBO Be God's sonties, 'twill be a hard way to hit! Can you tell me   35
  whether one Lancelot that dwells with him, dwell with him or
  no?
LANCELOT Talk you of young Master Lancelot? [*Aside*] Mark me now,
  now will I raise the waters. Talk you of young Master Lancelot?
GOBBO No 'master', sir, but a poor man's son. His father, though I   40
  say't, is an honest, exceeding poor man and, God be thanked, well
  to live.
LANCELOT Well, let his father be what a will, we talk of young Master
  Lancelot.
GOBBO Your worship's friend and Lancelot, sir.   45
LANCELOT But I pray you, *ergo* old man, *ergo* I beseech you, talk you
  of young Master Lancelot?
GOBBO Of Lancelot, an't please your mastership.
LANCELOT *Ergo* Master Lancelot. Talk not of Master Lancelot, father,
  for the young gentleman, according to fates and destinies, and such   50
  odd sayings, the sisters three, and such branches of learning, is
  indeed deceased, or as you would say in plain terms, gone to
  heaven.

After several attempts, Lancelot convinces his father that he is indeed talking to his own son. Lancelot plans to enter the service of Bassanio.

1 Stage 'business' (in pairs)

Actors often invent stage 'business' (actions, gestures) to help modern audiences understand language and jokes which are no longer clear. There are some expressions opposite with which a modern audience often needs help. Work out what 'business' could be added to the following to bring out their humour:

- 'Do I look like a cudgel or a hovel-post, a staff or a prop?' (line 56)
- 'Thou has got more hair on thy chin than Dobbin my fill-horse has on his tail' (lines 77–8)
- 'I have brought him a present' (line 83 – see line 111)
- 'Give him a halter!' (line 86)
- 'you may tell every finger I have with my ribs' (lines 87–8).

Show your ideas to the rest of the class.

2 Lancelot: a choice of writing activities

Either imagine you are Lancelot writing home to your father just after entering Shylock's service. Look at lines 85–92 for clues to what you might report. Add extra details as appropriate.

Or write a paragraph explaining what Lancelot's remark 'for I am a Jew if I serve the Jew any longer' (lines 91–2) suggests to you about the attitude of the poor people of Venice towards the Jews.

---

staff of my age   support in my old age
hovel-post   post to hold up a shelter
fill-horse   carthorse

set up my rest   determined
halter   noose to hang himself
liveries   uniforms

GOBBO Marry, God forbid! The boy was the very staff of my age, my
very prop. 55

LANCELOT Do I look like a cudgel or a hovel-post, a staff or a prop?
Do you know me, father?

GOBBO Alack the day, I know you not, young gentleman, but I pray
you tell me, is my boy – God rest his soul! – alive or dead?

LANCELOT Do you not know me, father? 60

GOBBO Alack, sir, I am sand-blind, I know you not.

LANCELOT Nay indeed, if you had your eyes you might fail of the
knowing me: it is a wise father that knows his own child. Well, old
man, I will tell you news of your son. [*Kneels*] Give me your
blessing; truth will come to light, murder cannot be hid long, a 65
man's son may, but in the end truth will out.

GOBBO Pray you, sir, stand up; I am sure you are not Lancelot my
boy.

LANCELOT Pray you, let's have no more fooling about it, but give me
your blessing; I am Lancelot your boy that was, your son that is, 70
your child that shall be.

GOBBO I cannot think you are my son.

LANCELOT I know not what I shall think of that; but I am Lancelot the
Jew's man, and I am sure Margery your wife is my mother.

GOBBO Her name is Margery indeed. I'll be sworn if thou be Lancelot 75
thou art mine own flesh and blood. Lord worshipped might he be,
what a beard hast thou got! Thou has got more hair on thy chin
than Dobbin my fill-horse has on his tail.

LANCELOT It should seem then that Dobbin's tail grows backward. I
am sure he had more hair of his tail than I have of my face when 80
I last saw him.

GOBBO Lord, how art thou changed! How dost thou and thy master
agree? I have brought him a present. How 'gree you now?

LANCELOT Well, well; but for mine own part, as I have set up my rest
to run away, so I will not rest till I have run some ground. My 85
master's a very Jew. Give him a present? Give him a halter! I am
famished in his service; you may tell every finger I have with my
ribs. Father, I am glad you are come; give me your present to one
Master Bassanio, who indeed gives rare new liveries: if I serve not
him, I will run as far as God has any ground. O rare fortune, here 90
comes the man! To him, father, for I am a Jew if I serve the Jew
any longer.

Bassanio sends a servant to fetch Gratiano. Lancelot and his father try to persuade Bassanio to employ Lancelot. Bassanio says that Shylock has already recommended Lancelot to him.

1 Two people trying to tell the same story (in pairs)

Take parts and read aloud Lancelot and Gobbo's lines 97–115 so that each speech follows on quickly from the other. Stress the comedy and confusion that arise when two characters compete in telling the same story, trying to speak at the same time, and when one of them is almost blind and cannot see the other's actions and reactions!

2 Language matters

a **Malapropisms**   A malapropism is 'a comical confusion of words', usually when a person chooses the wrong word in mistake for another that sounds like it. Gobbo uses several between lines 103 and 118. Find them and write down the words he really meant to use. Make up some sentences of your own that include malapropisms.

   (Malapropisms are named after Mrs Malaprop, who muddled up her language in Sheridan's play *The Rivals* (1775). Shakespeare would have known malapropisms as **cacozelia**.)

b **Prose and verse**   You will probably have already noticed that the language of the play quite often changes between verse and prose. Opposite, Bassanio shifts from speaking prose to verse (lines 119–23). Turn to page 183 to read about Shakespeare's use of verse and prose, and then suggest several possible reasons why he makes the change here.

3 A racist proverb? (in pairs)

Lancelot thanks Bassanio for employing him by delivering another criticism of Shylock (lines 124–6). He suggests that Christians have 'the grace of God' whereas Shylock has 'enough' (wealth). Talk together about whether you think this is another example of Christian prejudice against Jews in Venice.

---

anon   at once
Gramercy   God have mercy
aught   anything
scarce cater-cousins   hardly close
 friends

preferred   recommended
The old proverb   'The grace of God is
 gear enough' (God's grace is sufficient)
parted   divided
enough   wealth

Enter BASSANIO *with* [LEONARDO *and*] *a follower or two*

BASSANIO You may do so, but let it be so hasted that supper be ready
at the farthest by five of the clock. See these letters delivered, put
the liveries to making, and desire Gratiano to come anon to my   95
lodging.
                                                    [*Exit one of his men*]

LANCELOT To him, father.

GOBBO God bless your worship!

BASSANIO Gramercy; wouldst thou aught with me?

GOBBO Here's my son, sir, a poor boy –   100

LANCELOT Not a poor boy, sir, but the rich Jew's man that would, sir,
as my father shall specify –

GOBBO He hath a great infection, sir, as one would say, to serve –

LANCELOT Indeed, the short and the long is, I serve the Jew, and have
a desire, as my father shall specify –   105

GOBBO His master and he, saving your worship's reverence, are scarce
cater-cousins –

LANCELOT To be brief, the very truth is that the Jew having done me
wrong doth cause me – as my father being I hope an old man shall
frutify unto you –   110

GOBBO I have here a dish of doves that I would bestow upon your
worship, and my suit is –

LANCELOT In very brief, the suit is impertinent to myself, as your
worship shall know by this honest old man, and though I say it,
though old man, yet poor man, my father –   115

BASSANIO One speak for both. What would you?

LANCELOT Serve you, sir.

GOBBO That is the very defect of the matter, sir.

BASSANIO I know thee well, thou hast obtained thy suit.
    Shylock thy master spoke with me this day,   120
    And hath preferred thee, if it be preferment
    To leave a rich Jew's service to become
    The follower of so poor a gentleman.

LANCELOT The old proverb is very well parted between my master
Shylock and you, sir: you have the grace of God, sir, and he hath   125
enough.

Lancelot welcomes the prospect of serving Bassanio, who plans to entertain Antonio that night. Gratiano wishes to travel with Bassanio to Belmont. Bassanio advises him to improve his rough manners.

1 'Give him a livery' – what will Lancelot wear?

From now on, Lancelot will belong to Bassanio's household. Design a costume ('livery') for Lancelot to wear as Bassanio's servant.

2 Lancelot the fortune-teller (in pairs)

Lancelot fancies himself as a fortune-teller as he reads his own palm. Speak his lines 132–9 to discover what he predicts for himself. Then consider: if he had the chance to read the palms of some of the other characters, what might he foretell? One person plays Lancelot; the other chooses to be Shylock, Antonio, Bassanio or Portia.

Take it in turns to be Lancelot and the person having their fortune told. Base your predictions on what you know of the play so far. As you read on, see if any of your predictions come true.

3 Bassanio's baggage

Bassanio is preparing for the trip to Belmont. He orders Leonardo to buy certain items and then pack them: 'These things being bought and orderly bestowed' (line 142). If you were Bassanio, what would you take with you on the ship? Think carefully about why he is actually going to Belmont; then write your list.

4 Bassanio's fears about Gratiano (in pairs)

Read Bassanio's lines 151–60 to each other. He expresses concern that Gratiano's wild behaviour, although acceptable in the male-dominated Venetian world, will spoil his courtship of Portia. Emphasise key words, then improvise one example of Gratiano's behaviour ('too wild, too rude, and bold of voice') that has prompted Bassanio's concern.

---

guarded elaborate
fairer table luckier palm
coming-in beginning
'scape escape
'scapes adventures
gear matter

best esteemed acquaintance best friend
suit favour to ask
Parts characteristics
liberal free, licentious, over-the-top
misconstered misinterpreted

BASSANIO Thou speak'st it well; go, father, with thy son;
        Take leave of thy old master, and enquire
        My lodging out. [*To a follower*] Give him a livery
        More guarded than his fellows'; see it done.   130
LANCELOT Father, in. I cannot get a service, no, I have ne'er a tongue
in my head! [*Looks at palm of his hand*] Well, if any man in Italy
have a fairer table which doth offer to swear upon a book! – I shall
have good fortune. Go to, here's a simple line of life, here's a
small trifle of wives: alas, fifteen wives is nothing, eleven widows   135
and nine maids is a simple coming-in for one man. And then to
'scape drowning thrice, and to be in peril of my life with the edge
of a featherbed: here are simple 'scapes. Well, if Fortune be a
woman, she's a good wench for this gear. Father, come, I'll take my
leave of the Jew in the twinkling.   140
                    Exeunt Lancelot [and Gobbo]
BASSANIO I pray thee, good Leonardo, think on this.
        These things being bought and orderly bestowed,
        Return in haste, for I do feast tonight
        My best esteemed acquaintance. Hie thee, go.
LEONARDO My best endeavours shall be done herein.   145

       Enter GRATIANO

GRATIANO Where's your master?
LEONARDO   Yonder, sir, he walks.   *Exit*
GRATIANO Signor Bassanio!
BASSANIO Gratiano?
GRATIANO I have a suit to you.
BASSANIO   You have obtained it.
GRATIANO You must not deny me, I must go with you to Belmont.   150
BASSANIO Why then, you must. But hear thee, Gratiano:
        Thou art too wild, too rude, and bold of voice –
        Parts that become thee happily enough,
        And in such eyes as ours appear not faults;
        But where thou art not known, why there they show   155
        Something too liberal. Pray thee take pain
        To allay with some cold drops of modesty
        Thy skipping spirit, lest through thy wild behaviour
        I be misconstered in the place I go to,
        And lose my hopes.

Gratiano promises to behave respectably in Belmont – but not tonight! In Scene 3, Jessica laments Lancelot's imminent departure. She hands him a letter to give secretly to Lorenzo.

1 'Put on a sober habit' (in pairs)

Once again, Gratiano talks about playing a part: in lines 160–8 he promises to behave himself. Remember he has already offered to 'play the Fool' for Antonio (Act 1 Scene 1, line 79). But in lines 172–4 Bassanio urges Gratiano not to change his behaviour until they have left Venice for Belmont.

Choose one of Gratiano's examples of polite behaviour. Mime it. Can your partner guess which one you have chosen?

Talk together about whether you think Bassanio and Gratiano are being hypocritical in agreeing that Gratiano puts on an act in Belmont but is his usual raucous self in Venice.

2 Jessica's home life (in pairs)

Scene 3 is very short, and reveals Jessica's unhappiness at home: 'Our house is hell'. Only Lancelot's joking relieves the misery. Take parts as Jessica and Lancelot and read the whole scene. Change roles and read through again. Then try one of the following activities:

a Devise a series of three tableaux which you think capture some of the reasons for Jessica's unhappiness.

b As Jessica, each person writes a letter to the problem page of a teenage magazine. Describe the problems you have at home, and ask if you are right to desert your father for Lorenzo and convert to Christianity. Read each other's letters and make up suitable replies.

c Draw up two columns, one headed 'Jessica' and the other 'Portia'. Enter in each column what you have so far discovered about them. What similarities and differences can you identify?

---

a sober habit serious behaviour
hood cover
civility manners
studied practised
ostent appearance
bar except

gauge judge
suit of mirth cheerful mood
ducat gold coin
exhibit inhibit (he chooses the wrong word)
pagan someone who is not a Christian

GRATIANO   Signor Bassanio, hear me: 160
            If I do not put on a sober habit,
            Talk with respect, and swear but now and then,
            Wear prayer books in my pocket, look demurely,
            Nay more, while grace is saying, hood mine eyes
            Thus with my hat, and sigh and say 'amen',   165
            Use all the observance of civility
            Like one well studied in a sad ostent
            To please his grandam, never trust me more.
BASSANIO Well, we shall see your bearing.
GRATIANO Nay, but I bar tonight, you shall not gauge me   170
            By what we do tonight.
BASSANIO   No, that were pity.
            I would entreat you rather to put on
            Your boldest suit of mirth, for we have friends
            That purpose merriment. But fare you well,
            I have some business.   175
GRATIANO And I must to Lorenzo and the rest;
            But we will visit you at supper time.

                                                          Exeunt

Act 2 Scene 3
Venice

                Enter JESSICA and LANCELOT the Clown

JESSICA I am sorry thou wilt leave my father so.
            Our house is hell, and thou a merry devil
            Didst rob it of some taste of tediousness.
            But fare thee well: there is a ducat for thee.
            And, Lancelot, soon at supper shalt thou see   5
            Lorenzo, who is thy new master's guest;
            Give him this letter, do it secretly.
            And so farewell: I would not have my father
            See me in talk with thee.
LANCELOT Adieu; tears exhibit my tongue. Most beautiful pagan,   10
            most sweet Jew, if a Christian do not play the knave and get thee,
            I am much deceived. But adieu; these foolish drops do something
            drown my manly spirit. Adieu!   [*Exit*]

Jessica, ashamed to be Shylock's daughter, plans to marry Lorenzo and become a Christian. In Scene 4, arrangements for a masque are made. Lancelot delivers Jessica's letter.

---

1 How to stage Jessica's exit? (in pairs)

You will now have read all of Scene 3. Think about Jessica's state of mind as she says her lines. Work together to discover a dramatically convincing way for her to leave the stage, concentrating on the exact impression you wish to create for an audience. Show the version you like best to other groups.

2 The masque (in groups of five)

The four men plan to attend a masque (an entertainment with music, torches, dancing and elaborate masks and disguises). They must all wear disguises, as was the custom. The disguise might be a mask, a costume, or both. Read the whole scene first, then in groups try the following activities:

a **'Disguise us'**   Choose one character each and produce a disguise which reflects his personality. Display your ideas.

b **'Hold here, take this'**   'This' in line 19 might be a tip for Lancelot, the go-between, or it could be a gift for Jessica. Talk about the kind of gift Lorenzo might want to send to Jessica. Give reasons for your choice.

c **Director's notes**   As if you were directing the play, write a series of detailed notes for your character, explaining how this scene should be played. Look out for clues about the time of day and the characters' changing moods. How will you handle the various entrances and exits?

---

heinous dreadful
strife divided feelings (duty and love)

quaintly ordered carefully organised
break up unseal
hand handwriting

JESSICA Farewell, good Lancelot.

        Alack, what heinous sin is it in me   15

        To be ashamed to be my father's child!

        But though I am a daughter to his blood

        I am not to his manners. O Lorenzo,

        If thou keep promise, I shall end this strife,

        Become a Christian and thy loving wife.   *Exit*   20

Act 2 Scene 4
Venice

Enter GRATIANO, LORENZO, SALARINO, *and* SOLANIO

LORENZO Nay, we will slink away in supper time,

        Disguise us at my lodging, and return

        All in an hour.

GRATIANO We have not made good preparation.

SALARINO We have not spoke us yet of torchbearers.   5

SOLANIO 'Tis vile unless it may be quaintly ordered,

        And better in my mind not undertook.

LORENZO 'Tis now but four of clock; we have two hours

        To furnish us.

Enter LANCELOT [*with a letter*]

        Friend Lancelot! What's the news?

LANCELOT And it shall please you to break up this, it shall seem to   10
signify.

LORENZO I know the hand; in faith, 'tis a fair hand,

        And whiter than the paper it writ on

        Is the fair hand that writ.

GRATIANO   Love news, in faith!

LANCELOT By your leave, sir.   15

LORENZO Whither goest thou?

LANCELOT Marry, sir, to bid my old master the Jew to sup tonight
with my new master the Christian.

LORENZO Hold here, take this. Tell gentle Jessica

        I will not fail her; speak it privately.   20

        Exit Lancelot

Lorenzo tells Gratiano that Jessica plans to disguise herself as a boy and flee from Shylock, taking some of his gold and jewels. Scene 5 begins with Shylock talking of his generosity to Lancelot.

1 Jessica's plan – Lorenzo's reaction (in pairs)

Read Lorenzo's lines 29–39 aloud to each other. They tell of Jessica's plan to elope with Lorenzo and Lorenzo's reaction to it.

One person steps into role as Jessica, and tells in their own words the details of the elopement plan. After hearing that, the other person as Lorenzo gives his thoughts on the plan, including the attraction of the 'gold and jewels' that Jessica plans to take with her, and his attitude towards Shylock and his Jewish faith.

When Jessica appears Shylock hands her the keys of his house and sternly warns her to keep all doors and windows locked. Does Jessica's expression here show that she has planned to betray her father, stealing his money and eloping with Lorenzo?

page a young male servant	**gourmandise** over-eat
foot path	**rend apparel out** wear clothes out by
issue child	tearing them
faithless lacking the Christian faith	**was wont to tell** often told

Go, gentlemen:
Will you prepare you for this masque tonight?
I am provided of a torchbearer.

SALARINO Ay marry, I'll be gone about it straight.

SOLANIO And so will I.

LORENZO   Meet me and Gratiano   25
At Gratiano's lodging some hour hence.

SALARINO 'Tis good we do so.

Exeunt [Salarino and Solanio]

GRATIANO Was not that letter from fair Jessica?

LORENZO I must needs tell thee all. She hath directed
How I shall take her from her father's house,   30
What gold and jewels she is furnished with,
What page's suit she hath in readiness.
If e'er the Jew her father come to heaven,
It will be for his gentle daughter's sake;
And never dare misfortune cross her foot,   35
Unless she do it under this excuse
That she is issue to a faithless Jew.
Come, go with me; peruse this as thou goest.
Fair Jessica shall be my torchbearer.

Exeunt

Act 2 Scene 5
Venice   Shylock's house

Enter SHYLOCK *and* LANCELOT

SHYLOCK Well, thou shalt see, thy eyes shall be thy judge,
The difference of old Shylock and Bassanio –
What, Jessica! – Thou shalt not gourmandise
As thou hast done with me – What, Jessica! –
And sleep, and snore, and rend apparel out.   5
Why, Jessica, I say!

LANCELOT   Why, Jessica!

SHYLOCK Who bids thee call? I do not bid thee call.

LANCELOT Your worship was wont to tell me I could do nothing
without bidding.

Shylock intends to dine with Bassanio, even though he is uneasy because of ominous dreams. He leaves Jessica to protect the house, warning her not to watch the masque. Lancelot tells her of Lorenzo's impending visit.

1 'I am right loath to go': Shylock's apprehension (in groups of three)

Shylock is reluctant to go and dine with Bassanio. He assumes that they invite him only to 'flatter' him, and is nervous about leaving his house while the 'shallow foppery' of the masque goes on outside. Read the whole scene. Then try the following:

a One person reads Shylock's two speeches (lines 11–18 and lines 27–38). The others echo any words which reflect Shylock's nervous excitement. Which words seem particularly important in creating his agitated mood?

b Shylock angrily describes how he expects the Christians to behave during the masque (lines 27–38). Suggest reasons why he is so much against such behaviour.

   Pick out other examples from these two speeches of Shylock's disapproval of the Christians' attitudes and practices.

c Is Shylock a spoilsport? Discuss whether you think Shakespeare is deliberately or unfairly trying to make the audience dislike Shylock.

d In Shakespeare's time Shylock's 'dream of money bags' represented a vision of loss, not profit. But it causes problems for a modern audience because it seems to define Shylock as a money-obsessed stereotype. Line 18 is often cut in modern productions. Would you cut it? Why, or why not?

2 'Look to my house'

Shylock is very conscious of the need to keep his house locked and secure whilst he is away. Imagine that you are designing the set. How would you present Shylock's house on stage?

---

bid forth   invited
prodigal   wasteful
loath   unwilling
tonight   last night
reproach   approach (Lancelot's mistake, but Shylock takes him literally)

wry-necked fife   a flute (pretend to play a flute and see what happens to your neck)
with varnished faces   wearing masks
shallow foppery   hollow nonsense
Hagar's offspring   Ishmael, the outcast son of an Egyptian servant

Enter JESSICA

JESSICA Call you? What is your will?   10
SHYLOCK I am bid forth to supper, Jessica.
          There are my keys. But wherefore should I go?
          I am not bid for love, they flatter me;
          But yet I'll go in hate, to feed upon
          The prodigal Christian. Jessica my girl,   15
          Look to my house. I am right loath to go;
          There is some ill a-brewing towards my rest,
          For I did dream of money bags tonight.
LANCELOT I beseech you, sir, go; my young master doth expect your
     reproach.   20
SHYLOCK So do I his.
LANCELOT And they have conspired together – I will not say you shall
     see a masque; but if you do, then it was not for nothing that my
     nose fell a-bleeding on Black Monday last, at six a clock i'the
     morning, falling out that year on Ash Wednesday was four year in   25
     th'afternoon.
SHYLOCK What, are there masques? Hear you me, Jessica,
          Lock up my doors, and when you hear the drum
          And the vile squealing of the wry-necked fife,
          Clamber not you up to the casements then   30
          Nor thrust your head into the public street
          To gaze on Christian fools with varnished faces;
          But stop my house's ears – I mean my casements –
          Let not the sound of shallow foppery enter
          My sober house. By Jacob's staff I swear   35
          I have no mind of feasting forth tonight:
          But I will go. Go you before me, sirrah;
          Say I will come.
LANCELOT   I will go before, sir.
          [*Aside to Jessica*] Mistress, look out at window for all this:
          There will come a Christian by   40
          Will be worth a Jewès eye   [*Exit*]
SHYLOCK What says that fool of Hagar's offspring, ha?
JESSICA His words were 'Farewell, mistress', nothing else.

Shylock is glad to be rid of Lancelot, whom he sees as a lazy wastrel. Jessica relishes the prospect of escaping from her father. In Scene 6, Gratiano and Salarino await Lorenzo: he is late.

---

1 Impressions of Shylock (in groups of three)

Take parts as Shylock, Jessica and Lancelot and quickly reread Scene 5. Produce a visual wall chart on which you record the various impressions created of Shylock in his domestic setting. Display your work for other groups to look at.

2 Jessica's farewell – who loses most? (in small groups)

Jessica is going to leave her father and elope with Lorenzo. Make up a group tableau which captures the meaning of the final line of Scene 5. After your tableau talk together about who has the most to lose from this elopement: Jessica or Lorenzo? It will help your discussion if you bear in mind that these young people come from very different backgrounds.

3 Is the pleasure in the chase? (in small groups)

Like Salarino in lines 6–8, Gratiano (lines 9–20) talks of there being greater pleasure in the first anticipation of love than in its actual experience. Notice how he gives different examples to illustrate this theme. Read Gratiano's speech, changing reader at each punctuation mark. As you read, stress all the words to do with physical enjoyment and satisfaction. Talk about the effect you have achieved. Do you agree with what Salarino and Gratiano are saying? What do you think of their attitude towards women?

---

patch fool
Drones hive not bees that do not
 work will find no home
penthouse overhanging upper storey
make stand wait
O, ten times . . . unforfeited! the
 doves of love favour an engagement
 more than a long marriage

untread retrace
measures paces
unbated unrestrained
younger a young gentleman
scarfèd decked-out
strumpet prostitute
ribs ship's timbers
rent torn

SHYLOCK The patch is kind enough, but a huge feeder,
   Snail-slow in profit, and he sleeps by day   45
   More than the wildcat. Drones hive not with me,
   Therefore I part with him, and part with him
   To one that I would have him help to waste
   His borrowed purse. Well, Jessica, go in;
   Perhaps I will return immediately.   50
   Do as I bid you, shut doors after you.
   Fast bind, fast find:
   A proverb never stale in thrifty mind.   *Exit*
JESSICA Farewell, and if my fortune be not crossed,
   I have a father, you a daughter, lost.   *Exit* 55

Act 2 Scene 6
Venice Outside Shylock's house

Enter the masquers, GRATIANO and SALARINO

GRATIANO This is the penthouse under which Lorenzo
   Desired us to make stand.
SALARINO His hour is almost past.
GRATIANO And it is marvel he outdwells his hour,
   For lovers ever run before the clock.   5
SALARINO O, ten times faster Venus' pigeons fly
   To seal love's bonds new made than they are wont
   To keep obligèd faith unforfeited!
GRATIANO That ever holds: who riseth from a feast
   With that keen appetite that he sits down?   10
   Where is the horse that doth untread again
   His tedious measures with the unbated fire
   That he did pace them first? All things that are
   Are with more spirit chasèd than enjoyed.
   How like a younger or a prodigal   15
   The scarfèd bark puts from her native bay,
   Hugged and embracèd by the strumpet wind!
   How like the prodigal doth she return
   With overweathered ribs and ragged sails,
   Lean, rent, and beggared by the strumpet wind! 20

Lorenzo meets his friends outside Shylock's house. Jessica, although embarrassed by her disguise as a boy, is ready to elope with him, having already plundered her father's gold and jewels.

1 Late arrival (in pairs)

'My affairs have made you wait.' Lorenzo's late arrival is in contradiction to all Gratiano has just said about lovers. Suggest why Shakespeare makes Lorenzo late, and what he might have been doing whilst the others have been waiting.

2 A tender dialogue (in pairs)

Jessica, still in her father's house, talks to Lorenzo, who is in the street below. Take parts and read lines 27–51, but make sure that you are at some distance from each other. You could also place some kind of barrier or obstacle between you. First, read the lines as tenderly and romantically as possible, then try reading them to stress the physical awkwardness of the situation and the difficulties of communicating. Which version did you prefer?

3 Jessica: a woman in a man's world

a Make a list of all of Jessica's comments about herself and her assumed disguise as a boy in lines 34–51. Alongside each, write what they tell you of her character and what they suggest of the role of women in Venice.

b Jessica declares her love for Lorenzo, but she also ensures that she steals her own dowry (line 34) and that she goes back to plunder even more of her father's wealth before she elopes (lines 50–1). Write a paragraph on what this suggests about Jessica and about Venetian values.

---

long abode lateness
exchange disguise
light obvious (or wanton)
office of discovery act of
  revelation
garnish disguise or costume
close secretive

stayed for awaited
gild cover in gold
moe more
hood mask or hat
gentle a woman who has been well
  brought up (also a pun on 'gentile' – a
  non-Jew)

Enter LORENZO

SALARINO Here comes Lorenzo; more of this hereafter.
LORENZO Sweet friends, your patience for my long abode.
     Not I but my affairs have made you wait.
     When you shall please to play the thieves for wives,
     I'll watch as long for you then. Approach –   25
     Here dwells my father Jew. Ho! Who's within?

   [*Enter*] JESSICA *above*[, *in boy's clothes*]

JESSICA Who are you? Tell me, for more certainty,
     Albeit I'll swear that I do know your tongue.
LORENZO Lorenzo, and thy love.
JESSICA Lorenzo certain, and my love indeed,   30
     For who love I so much? And now who knows
     But you, Lorenzo, whether I am yours?
LORENZO Heaven and thy thoughts are witness that thou art.
JESSICA Here, catch this casket, it is worth the pains.
     I am glad 'tis night, you do not look on me,   35
     For I am much ashamed of my exchange.
     But love is blind, and lovers cannot see
     The pretty follies that themselves commit;
     For if they could, Cupid himself would blush
     To see me thus transformèd to a boy.   40
LORENZO Descend, for you must be my torchbearer.
JESSICA What, must I hold a candle to my shames?
     They in themselves, good sooth, are too too light.
     Why, 'tis an office of discovery, love,
     And I should be obscured.
LORENZO   So are you, sweet,   45
     Even in the lovely garnish of a boy.
     But come at once,
     For the close night doth play the runaway,
     And we are stayed for at Bassanio's feast.
JESSICA I will make fast the doors, and gild myself   50
     With some moe ducats, and be with you straight.
                  [*Exit Jessica above*]
GRATIANO Now by my hood, a gentle and no Jew!

Lorenzo talks of his love for Jessica, then elopes with her. Antonio informs Gratiano that Bassanio's ship is about to leave. In Scene 7, the prince of Morocco considers which casket to choose.

---

1 Well done, Jessica – or . . .? (in pairs)

Both Gratiano and Lorenzo applaud Jessica's actions in betraying her father. Lorenzo's lines 53–8 are fulsome in their admiration of his prospective wife but his words are full of unconscious irony (a deeper level of meaning than he may intend to convey). For example, his use of the word 'if' might suggest he still harbours some doubts about Jessica. One reads the speech aloud; the other picks out words or comments that have ironic possibilities.

2 Jessica's letter to Shylock

Imagine that Jessica writes a letter to her father for him to discover when she has left. What's in it?

3 The casket scene (in groups of any size)

This is the first of the casket scenes. In performance, the disclosure of the caskets is often staged with elaborate dignity and a strong sense of ceremony.

a **The caskets** Jot down some first impressions about what the caskets might look like. There is an activity and information about them on page 72.

b **How do they enter?** At the beginning of Scene 7, Portia and Morocco enter with their trains (followers). Talk about how you think the opening three lines should be staged. Should Portia and Morocco enter separately or together? Where do they position themselves to await the unveiling of the caskets? Then try the entrance and unveiling practically in several different ways. Choose which you felt worked best.

c **Keeping an eye on Portia** Portia's opening speech (lines 1–3) is simple and direct, recognising the formality of the situation. She speaks in simple commands ('draw', 'discover', 'make') and her words give little away about what she's feeling. Imagine that she could voice her private thoughts (an interior monologue) at line 3. What would she be thinking?

Beshrew me Devil take me (a mild oath)

is come about has changed
several different

LORENZO Beshrew me but I love her heartily.
      For she is wise, if I can judge of her,
      And fair she is, if that mine eyes be true,   55
      And true she is, as she hath proved herself:
      And therefore like herself, wise, fair, and true,
      Shall she be placèd in my constant soul.

Enter JESSICA

      What, art thou come? On, gentleman, away!
      Our masquing mates by this time for us stay.
                                  Exit [*with Jessica*]

Enter ANTONIO

ANTONIO Who's there?
GRATIANO Signor Antonio?
ANTONIO Fie, fie, Gratiano, where are all the rest?
      'Tis nine a clock, our friends all stay for you.
      No masque tonight: the wind is come about,   65
      Bassanio presently will go aboard.
      I have sent twenty out to seek for you.
GRATIANO I am glad on't; I desire no more delight
      Than to be under sail and gone tonight.
                                    Exeunt

Act 2 Scene 7
Belmont   A room in Portia's house

Enter PORTIA *with the Prince of* MOROCCO *and both their trains*

PORTIA Go, draw aside the curtains and discover
      The several caskets to this noble prince.
      Now make your choice.
MOROCCO This first of gold, who this inscription bears,
      'Who chooseth me, shall gain what many men desire.'   5
      The second silver, which this promise carries,
      'Who chooseth me, shall get as much as he deserves.'
      This third dull lead, with warning all as blunt,
      'Who chooseth me, must give and hazard all he hath.'
      How shall I know if I do choose the right?   10

Portia reminds Morocco that he can win her hand by choosing the correct casket. Morocco deliberates over the three choices: lead, silver and gold.

---

1 Morocco ♡ Portia? (in small groups)

First, try a group reading of Morocco's lines 13–60. Each person reads as far as the next punctuation mark, then hands on to the next reader. Then choose one or more of the following activities:

a Reread the speech, echoing all the references that Morocco makes to himself. What is the effect?

b Talk together about whether you think he is 'over the top'. Do you think that Morocco exaggerates too much?

c In lines 39–48, Morocco talks extravagantly about the extremes to which men go to woo Portia. Speak the lines as pompously as you can, adding gestures.

d Talk together about how you would stage this soliloquy.

e Choose two moments in the speech when you could add to Portia's interior monologue (see Activity 3c, p. 56). One could be based on the picture below.

---

withal as well
dross worthless things
even unbiased
estimation reputation
disabling undervaluing

graved engraved
Hyrcanian deserts open land near the Caspian Sea
throughfares highways
watery kingdom the sea

PORTIA The one of them contains my picture, prince.
 If you choose that, then I am yours withal.
MOROCCO Some god direct my judgement! Let me see:
 I will survey th'inscriptions back again.
 What says this leaden casket?   15
 'Who chooseth me, must give and hazard all he hath.'
 Must give – for what? For lead? Hazard for lead!
 This casket threatens: men that hazard all
 Do it in hope of fair advantages.
 A golden mind stoops not to shows of dross;   20
 I'll then nor give nor hazard aught for lead.
 What says the silver with her virgin hue?
 'Who chooseth me, shall get as much as he deserves.'
 As much as he deserves – pause there, Morocco,
 And weigh thy value with an even hand.   25
 If thou be'st rated by thy estimation
 Thou dost deserve enough; and yet enough
 May not extend so far as to the lady;
 And yet to be afeared of my deserving
 Were but a weak disabling of myself.   30
 As much as I deserve: why, that's the lady.
 I do in birth deserve her, and in fortunes,
 In graces, and in qualities of breeding:
 But more than these, in love I do deserve.
 What if I strayed no farther, but chose here?   35
 Let's see once more this saying graved in gold:
 'Who chooseth me, shall gain what many men desire.'
 Why, that's the lady; all the world desires her.
 From the four corners of the earth they come
 To kiss this shrine, this mortal breathing saint.   40
 The Hyrcanian deserts and the vasty wilds
 Of wide Arabia are as throughfares now
 For princes to come view fair Portia.
 The watery kingdom, whose ambitious head
 Spits in the face of heaven, is no bar   45
 To stop the foreign spirits, but they come
 As o'er a brook to see fair Portia.
 One of these three contains her heavenly picture.

Morocco decides to open the gold casket, hoping to discover Portia's picture inside. However, he finds only a skull and a dismissive message. To Portia's relief, Morocco departs for home.

---

1 What's inside the casket? (in pairs)

After all his confident declamations Morocco opens the gold casket to find a human skull inside. He removes a scroll, with a message on it, from inside one of the eye sockets (see top picture on p. vii). Try one or more of the following activities:

a **Why a skull?** Discuss the possible reasons for Shakespeare including the skull. Then make a drawing of the casket's contents.

b **'All that glisters is not gold'** Line 65 is one of the best-known lines in the play, and is often used as a proverb today.

  • Did you think it was inevitable that Morocco would choose the gold casket? Give reasons for your answer.
  • Which other characters might well need reminding of this saying? Again, give reasons for your response.

c **Write a message *from* Morocco** Read aloud the words on the scroll (lines 65–73), stressing the rhyme at the end of each line. Then write your own nine-line poem in a similar style, using as your theme Morocco's response to the message on the scroll. You will need to choose a very common word ending that has lots of possibilities for rhyming.

2 'Let all of his complexion choose me so' (in groups of three or four)

Portia's final line could well cause offence to an audience for its racism. If you were directing the play, would you include it or leave it out? Give reasons for your choice, and say how the line adds to your impression of Portia.

---

like likely
rib enclose
cerecloth shroud, a cloth in which a corpse was wrapped
immured walled up
tried purified

insculped engraved
thrive prosper
form likeness, picture
carrion death bare skull
inscrolled written down
tedious long-drawn-out

Is't like that lead contains her? 'Twere damnation
To think so base a thought; it were too gross   50
To rib her cerecloth in the òbscure grave.
Or shall I think in silver she's immured,
Being ten times undervalued to tried gold?
O sinful thought! Never so rich a gem
Was set in worse than gold. They have in England   55
A coin that bears the figure of an angel
Stampèd in gold; but that's insculped upon:
But here an angel in a golden bed
Lies all within. Deliver me the key:
Here do I choose, and thrive I as I may.   60
PORTIA   There take it, prince, and if my form lie there,
Then I am yours.
             [Morocco unlocks the gold casket]
MOROCCO   O hell! What have we here?
A carrion death, within whose empty eye
There is a written scroll. I'll read the writing.
    'All that glisters is not gold;   65
    Often have you heard that told.
    Many a man his life hath sold
    But my outside to behold.
    Gilded tombs do worms infold.
    Had you been as wise as bold,   70
    Young in limbs, in judgement old,
    Your answer had not been inscrolled.
    Fare you well, your suit is cold.'
Cold indeed, and labour lost;
Then farewell heat, and welcome frost.   75
Portia, adieu; I have too grieved a heart
To take a tedious leave: thus losers part.
                   Exit [Morocco with his train]
PORTIA   A gentle riddance! Draw the curtains, go.
Let all of his complexion choose me so.
                Exeunt. [A flourish of cornets]

Bassanio and Gratiano have sailed for Belmont. Jessica, having taken money and jewels, has eloped with Lorenzo. Solanio tells of Shylock's intense anguish at his loss, and suggests that he will seek revenge.

1 Loss after loss . . . (in pairs)

Another short scene increases dramatic tension. Just as the previous scene ended with a loser, Shakespeare now dramatises reports of two other losers. Salarino and Solanio tell of Shylock's grief at the loss of his daughter, hint at a lost ship, then tell of Antonio's sadness at parting from Bassanio. To first of all gain a sense of the whole scene, take parts and read through.

2 'With outcries raised the Duke' (in pairs)

Shylock visits the Duke of Venice to complain about the loss of his daughter and his possessions. He seeks support from the laws of Venice. Shylock manages to persuade the Duke to go with him, intending to search Bassanio's ship.

Improvise Shylock's meeting with the Duke. Concentrate on the reasons why Shylock is aggrieved, his state of mind, and how the Duke receives him.

3 Sympathy for Shylock? (in groups of five or six)

Solanio and Salarino report what has happened to Shylock (lines 12–24). Take it in turns to be Shylock, and use as many of his own words as possible. The others follow Shylock round the room, mocking and taunting him by ridiculing his words and actions. Everyone should take a turn as Shylock.

Afterwards, talk about how you felt as Shylock and what this tells you about his predicament.

Neither Salarino nor Solanio has any sympathy for Shylock. Solanio calls him 'The villain Jew' and 'the dog Jew' rather than mention his name. They mock his response to his losses. How do you feel towards them?

---

certified	testified to	**part**	separate
passion	emotional outburst	**miscarrièd**	was wrecked
keep his day	fulfil his bond	**fraught**	laden
reasoned	chatted		

Act 2 Scene 8
Venice

Enter SALARINO and SOLANIO

SALARINO Why, man, I saw Bassanio under sail,
With him is Gratiano gone along;
And in their ship I am sure Lorenzo is not.

SOLANIO The villain Jew with outcries raised the Duke,
Who went with him to search Bassanio's ship.   5

SALARINO He came too late, the ship was under sail.
But there the Duke was given to understand
That in a gondola were seen together
Lorenzo and his amorous Jessica.
Besides, Antonio certified the Duke   10
They were not with Bassanio in his ship.

SOLANIO I never heard a passion so confused,
So strange, outrageous, and so variable,
As the dog Jew did utter in the streets:
'My daughter! O my ducats! O my daughter!   15
Fled with a Christian! O my Christian ducats!
Justice! The law! My ducats and my daughter!
A sealèd bag, two sealèd bags of ducats,
Of double ducats, stolen from me by my daughter!
And jewels – two stones, two rich and precious stones,   20
Stolen by my daughter! Justice! Find the girl!
She hath the stones upon her and the ducats!'

SALARINO Why, all the boys in Venice follow him,
Crying his stones, his daughter, and his ducats.

SOLANIO Let good Antonio look he keep his day,   25
Or he shall pay for this.

SALARINO Marry, well remembered:
I reasoned with a Frenchman yesterday
Who told me, in the Narrow Seas that part
The French and English, there miscarrièd   30
A vessel of our country richly fraught.

Salarino hopes that the shipwrecked galleon was not one of Antonio's. He describes the selfless and loving friendship Antonio has for Bassanio. Scene 9 prepares for the prince of Arragon's choice of casket.

---

1 Sixty-second newsflash (in small groups)

You are a reporter for Radio Venice. Compose a brief newsflash on the shipwreck in 'the Narrow Seas' (line 29). You could include interviews with the Frenchman who told Salarino about it, and with Salarino himself. Your report must be no longer than sixty seconds.

2 'I saw Bassanio and Antonio part' (in groups of three)

As one person reads lines 37–50, the other two enact the parting of Bassanio and Antonio, showing all the details described. Can you work out different ways of presenting line 48?

3 Shylock versus Antonio

Scene 8 gives a dramatic impression of the differences between Shylock and Antonio, especially in terms of how they handle the 'loss' of what is dear to them. Make two columns, headed 'Shylock' and 'Antonio', and produce a list of all the contrasting details you can find. Include as much of Shakespeare's language as possible.

When you have completed your lists, review them in the light of the fact that all the information comes from two Christians who are friends of Antonio and detest Shylock. How does that affect your interpretation of the differences between Shylock and Antonio? How trustworthy are Salarino and Solanio's accounts?

Slubber   perform in a slovenly way
the very . . . time   until you have
 fulfilled your intentions
ostents   displays
affection wondrous sensible   very
 strong emotion

quicken   enliven
tane   taken
election   choice
presently   at once

I thought upon Antonio when he told me,
And wished in silence that it were not his.

SOLANIO You were best to tell Antonio what you hear.
Yet do not suddenly, for it may grieve him. 35

SALARINO A kinder gentleman treads not the earth.
I saw Bassanio and Antonio part:
Bassanio told him he would make some speed
Of his return: he answered, 'Do not so.
Slubber not business for my sake, Bassanio, 40
But stay the very riping of the time;
And for the Jew's bond which he hath of me,
Let it not enter in your mind of love.
Be merry, and employ your chiefest thoughts
To courtship, and such fair ostents of love 45
As shall conveniently become you there.'
And even there, his eye being big with tears,
Turning his face, he put his hand behind him,
And with affection wondrous sensible
He wrung Bassanio's hand, and so they parted. 50

SOLANIO I think he only loves the world for him.
I pray thee let us go and find him out
And quicken his embracèd heaviness
With some delight or other.

SALARINO   Do we so.

Exeunt

Act 2 Scene 9
Belmont   A room in Portia's house

Enter NERISSA and a Servitor

NERISSA Quick, quick, I pray thee, draw the curtain straight.
The Prince of Arragon hath tane his oath,
And comes to his election presently.

The prince of Arragon, hoping to win Portia, explains the terms of the oath he has undertaken. He deliberates about his choice of casket.

---

1 Portia: here we go again . . . (in small groups)

Morocco's choosing of the caskets was prefaced by a grand entrance of the prince and his followers (Act 2 Scene 1), which was matched by Portia and her train. Now she enters alone, even though Arragon is again accompanied by a procession of his companions. Consider how you would stage Portia's entrance in this scene. Then compare the dramatic effect created in this scene with that in Act 2 Scene 1.

2 What are the women thinking? (in pairs)

a Take it in turns to read aloud Arragon's long speech (lines 18–51), pausing at the end of each sentence. As one person reads, the other gives Portia's reaction to each sentence. Questions that will help you are:

- Does Portia already know in which casket her portrait is locked?
- How does she feel about the prospect of being married to Arragon?

b Nerissa is silent after the first three lines of the scene, but she observes all that goes on, and she knows Portia intimately. Together, write her developing thoughts as the choosing ceremony unfolds.

3 Newspaper report: draft, edit, final version (in pairs)

You are a news reporter with the *Belmont Gazette*. You have been instructed by your editor to cover Arragon's public courtship of Portia. You have a maximum of 200 words plus headline space. Summarise the main points made by Arragon in lines 18–51 as he considers which casket to choose. Comment on your impressions of him as a potential husband to Portia, the mistress of Belmont. Remain as true as you can to his actual words. Each person prepares a draft and swaps it with their partner's for comment and sub-editing. Each then rewrites their final copy.

---

nuptial rites marriage ceremony	**the martlet** the swift or house martin
unfold disclose	**casualty** misfortune
injunctions conditions	**jump** agree
addressed prepared	**cozen** cheat
ere before	**stamp of merit** genuine merit
fond foolish	

[A flourish of cornets.] Enter [the Prince of] ARRAGON, *his train,*
and PORTIA

PORTIA Behold, there stand the caskets, noble prince.
If you choose that wherein I am contained,   5
Straight shall our nuptial rites be solemnised;
But if you fail, without more speech, my lord,
You must be gone from hence immediately.

ARRAGON I am enjoined by oath to observe three things:
First, never to unfold to anyone   10
Which casket 'twas I chose; next, if I fail
Of the right casket, never in my life
To woo a maid in way of marriage; lastly,
If I do fail in fortune of my choice,
Immediately to leave you and be gone.   15

PORTIA To these injunctions everyone doth swear
That comes to hazard for my worthless self.

ARRAGON And so have I addressed me. Fortune now
To my heart's hope! Gold, silver, and base lead.
'Who chooseth me, must give and hazard all he hath.'   20
You shall look fairer ere I give or hazard.
What says the golden chest? Ha, let me see:
'Who chooseth me, shall gain what many men desire.'
What many men desire: that 'many' may be meant
By the fool multitude that choose by show,   25
Not learning more than the fond eye doth teach,
Which pries not to th'interior, but like the martlet
Builds in the weather on the outward wall,
Even in the force and road of casualty.
I will not choose what many men desire,   30
Because I will not jump with common spirits,
And rank me with the barbarous multitudes.
Why then, to thee, thou silver treasure house:
Tell me once more what title thou dost bear.
'Who chooseth me, shall get as much as he deserves.'   35
And well said too, for who shall go about
To cozen Fortune and be honourable
Without the stamp of merit? Let none presume
To wear an undeservèd dignity.

Arragon, guided by what he feels he deserves, chooses the silver casket. He finds the portrait of a 'blinking idiot' instead of Portia's picture. Disappointed, he takes his leave.

'What's here? The portrait of a blinking idiot'. To the delight of Portia and Jessica, Arragon chooses the silver casket, only to find himself mocked.

1 'Too long a pause . . .' (in pairs)

Read line 52 to each other in as many different ways as possible to convey Portia's thoughts and feelings. Decide which you think is the most appropriate and effective way, and why.

2 Just deserts?

Arragon, for all his pretentious self-importance, admits that he will go away not with one 'fool's head' but two, and that he will 'Patiently' bear his punishment. Does this redeem him in your eyes? Write a paragraph on what you think of him, and how he compares with Morocco.

---

estates, degrees, and offices   titles, qualifications and positions
cover   wear hats (as a sign of greatness)
that stand bare   who take off their hats / go bareheaded

gleaned   picked out and rejected
desert   what is my right
schedule   written scroll
distinct offices   separate functions
iwis   without doubt
wroth   anger and grief

O, that estates, degrees, and offices   40
Were not derived corruptly, and that clear honour
Were purchased by the merit of the wearer!
How many then should cover that stand bare!
How many be commanded that command!
How much low peasantry would then be gleaned   45
From the true seed of honour, and how much honour
Picked from the chaff and ruin of the times
To be new varnished! Well, but to my choice.
'Who chooseth me, shall get as much as he deserves.'
I will assume desert. Give me a key for this,   50
And instantly unlock my fortunes here.
                    [*Arragon unlocks the silver casket*]
PORTIA Too long a pause for that which you find there.
ARRAGON What's here? The portrait of a blinking idiot
          Presenting me a schedule! I will read it.
          How much unlike art thou to Portia!   55
          How much unlike my hopes and my deservings.
          'Who chooseth me, shall have as much as he deserves.'
          Did I deserve no more than a fool's head?
          Is that my prize? Are my deserts no better?
PORTIA To offend and judge are distinct offices,   60
          And of opposèd natures.
ARRAGON   What is here?
                    [*He reads*]
          'The fire seven times tried this;
          Seven times tried that judgement is
          That did never choose amiss.
          Some there be that shadows kiss;   65
          Such have but a shadow's bliss.
          There be fools alive iwis
          Silvered o'er, and so was this.
          Take what wife you will to bed,
          I will ever be your head.   70
          So be gone, you are sped.'
          Still more fool I shall appear
          By the time I linger here.
          With one fool's head I came to woo,
          But I go away with two.   75
          Sweet, adieu; I'll keep my oath,
          Patiently to bear my wroth.
                    [*Exit Arragon with his train*]

Portia is relieved that Arragon has chosen wrongly. A Messenger informs her that a new suitor has arrived from Venice. Nerissa, for Portia's sake, hopes that it is Bassanio.

---

1 Another jibe from Portia (in pairs)

Once more, when her suitor has left, Portia expresses her true feelings. She mocks Arragon as an insect (line 78) and another of the 'fools' who resort to excessive reasoning in pursuit of the answer to the casket riddle. Talk about what this adds to your impressions of Portia, then make notes in the file you are keeping on her.

2 News of Bassanio – a delayed ending (in pairs)

The scene could have ended with Nerissa drawing the curtain across the caskets, but it doesn't. Instead, a Messenger tells of the arrival of another lord wishing to seek Portia's hand in marriage. It seems this lord may be Bassanio.

a Talk together about why this 'delayed ending' is dramatically effective.

b One person reads the Messenger's lines 85–94. The other echoes all words which create a promising and positive picture of the new arrival.

c Contrast your impression of the third suitor with the presentation of Arragon and Morocco.

d The Messenger tells of gifts ('sensible regreets', line 88) for Portia on behalf of a Venetian lord. Nerissa and Portia both hope that it is Bassanio about to arrive at Belmont. What would be appropriate gifts for him to offer? Your ideas should reflect the characters of Bassanio and Portia, as well as the type of society depicted in the play.

---

deliberate   reasoning
They have . . . wit to lose   All their wisdom leads only to them choosing wrongly
sensible regreets   gifts
To wit   thus
commends   compliments
breath   words

likely   promising
costly   splendid
forespurrer   horseman who goes ahead of the others
kin   relation
highday wit   fine language
post   messenger
so mannerly   in such a fetching way

PORTIA Thus hath the candle singed the moth.
      O, these deliberate fools! When they do choose
      They have the wisdom by their wit to lose. 80
NERISSA The ancient saying is no heresy:
      'Hanging and wiving goes by destiny.'
PORTIA Come draw the curtain, Nerissa.

Enter a MESSENGER

MESSENGER Where is my lady?
PORTIA   Here. What would my lord?
MESSENGER Madam, there is alighted at your gate 85
      A young Venetian, one that comes before
      To signify th'approaching of his lord,
      From whom he bringeth sensible regreets:
      To wit, besides commends and courteous breath,
      Gifts of rich value. Yet I have not seen 90
      So likely an ambassador of love.
      A day in April never came so sweet
      To show how costly summer was at hand
      As this forespurrer comes before his lord.
PORTIA No more I pray thee, I am half afeared 95
      Thou wilt say anon he is some kin to thee,
      Thou spend'st such highday wit in praising him.
      Come, come, Nerissa, for I long to see
      Quick Cupid's post that comes so mannerly.
NERISSA Bassanio, Lord Love, if thy will it be! 100

                                   Exeunt

Looking back at Act 2
Activities for groups or individuals

---

1 Appearances can be deceptive . . .

Act 2 is full of instances when the truth is hidden or disguised. Identify as many examples as you can where appearance does not match reality (there are at least ten). When you have compiled your list, use it to write an essay titled 'How the theme of appearance versus reality is dramatised in Act 2'.

2 Love

Love is clearly a major theme of the play, but it manifests itself in different ways. For each of the nine scenes, write a sentence saying how you think it explores 'love' in some form or other. It won't be immediately evident in some scenes!

3 Fathers and daughters

Conflict between fathers and daughters occurs in many of Shakespeare's plays. *The Merchant of Venice* is no exception. In Act 2 both Portia and Jessica try to come to terms with the demands made on them by their fathers.

Explore this father–daughter conflict through a modern medium. Imagine you are producing a daytime TV chat show on 'fathers and daughters'. Interview Portia and Jessica as your special guests. You will need three people to do this; the rest of the class can be the studio audience. Encourage them to ask questions, too!

4 Design the caskets

Shakespeare never tells what the caskets are actually like. He leaves it to the imagination. In one production they were over six feet tall!

Draw or make your own version of the gold, silver and lead caskets. Think carefully about their shape, size and design. On pages 68 and 84 are examples of caskets used in two different productions of the play.

5 Restructuring the play

In many productions, Act 2 Scene 1 and Act 2 Scene 7 are put together and played as one continuous scene. What do you think are the dramatic advantages and disadvantages of playing the Morocco scenes in this way?

6 An extra scene

Shylock appears in only five scenes, but some directors give him a sixth which is not in the original script! This is a scene where Shylock returns from supper with the Christians to find that his daughter has deserted him and taken his valuables. In one such production Shylock returns, knocks, enters his house and rushes to all the windows. When he finds the house empty he flings himself on the ground, tears his clothes and sprinkles ashes on his head. Talk together about the value of adding such a scene.

7 Jessica and Shylock

Identify all the scenes which reveal something about Jessica's relationship with her father, and look again at the picture on page viii. Then consider:

- What signs are there of love and affection between father and daughter?
- What do you think of one director's decision to have Shylock actually strike Jessica during one of their exchanges?
- How do *you* see their relationship?

8 Jessica and Lorenzo

Study the picture. Is this how you see the relationship between Jessica and Lorenzo?

Solanio and Salarino talk of the rumours sweeping the Rialto about Antonio's ship wrecked on the Goodwin Sands. They taunt Shylock about Jessica's elopement. He suspects that they were part of the conspiracy.

1 Sixty-second newsflash (in pairs)

Using the details in lines 2–6, produce a radio newsflash about Antonio's latest piece of bad luck. It should be no longer than sixty seconds. If possible, tape-record your report to broadcast to the rest of the class.

2 What's in a name? (in small groups)

Solanio (lines 10–11) gives a warm and glowing tribute to 'the good Antonio, the honest Antonio'. Shylock (lines 17–18) is 'the devil . . . in the likeness of a Jew'. Talk together about the effects of denying Shylock his name.

3 Sympathy for Shylock? (in pairs)

In one production of the play, Shylock entered with Jessica's discarded dress in his arms. Talk about the effect this might have on the audience.

Think up your own ideas for Shylock's entry to give the audience an understanding of how he feels about Jessica's betrayal. How does he move? What are his facial expressions and physical appearance? What other meaningful object could he carry on stage? Talk through your ideas for making Shylock's entry dramatically powerful. Act out your suggestions.

4 Baiting Shylock (in groups of three)

Take parts and read lines 19–30. Try to find ways of bringing out the hostility of the Christians and Shylock's angry hurt (see picture at bottom of p. v).

---

flat sandbanks covered with shallow sea water
knapped ginger munched ginger
slips of prolixity exaggerations of a story
crossing . . . talk going into too much detail

O that . . . company! I wish my reputation was as good as his
cross spoil
complexion character
dam mother bird
Rebels . . . years? Can't you get an erection?

Act 3 Scene 1
Venice   A public place

Enter SOLANIO *and* SALARINO

SOLANIO Now, what news on the Rialto?

SALARINO Why, yet it lives there unchecked that Antonio hath a ship
of rich lading wrecked on the Narrow Seas; the Goodwins I think
they call the place – a very dangerous flat, and fatal, where the
carcases of many a tall ship lie buried, as they say, if my gossip   5
Report be an honest woman of her word.

SOLANIO I would she were as lying a gossip in that as ever knapped
ginger or made her neighbours believe she wept for the death of a
third husband. But it is true, without any slips of prolixity, or
crossing the plain highway of talk, that the good Antonio, the   10
honest Antonio – O that I had a title good enough to keep his name
company! –

SALARINO Come, the full stop.

SOLANIO Ha, what sayest thou? Why, the end is, he hath lost a
ship.   15

SALARINO I would it might prove the end of his losses.

SOLANIO Let me say 'amen' betimes, lest the devil cross my prayer,
for here he comes in the likeness of a Jew.

Enter SHYLOCK

How now, Shylock, what news among the merchants?

SHYLOCK You knew, none so well, none so well as you, of my daugh-   20
ter's flight.

SALARINO That's certain; I for my part knew the tailor that made the
wings she flew withal.

SOLANIO And Shylock for his own part knew the bird was fledged, and
then it is the complexion of them all to leave the dam.   25

SHYLOCK She is damned for it.

SALARINO That's certain – if the devil may be her judge.

SHYLOCK My own flesh and blood to rebel!

SOLANIO Out upon it, old carrion! Rebels it at these years?

SHYLOCK I say my daughter is my flesh and my blood.   30

Shylock speaks menacingly of Antonio and the bond between them. He stresses the common humanity of both Jews and Christians, and says he will learn from Christian example and seek revenge.

1 'I'm the same as you, so I'll do the same as you!' (in small groups)

Lines 42–57 are among the most famous in all Shakespeare. To explore Shylock's feelings, choose one or more of the following:

a Stand in a circle and read around the group, changing over at the end of each sentence. Make your first reading angry and revengeful. Then read it again quietly and with dignity, as a plea for understanding and common humanity.

b Two of you are Solanio and Salarino and stand at the opposite end of the room from the rest of the group. The others begin reading the speech in unison, moving towards the two Christians as they speak. Increase the volume the nearer you get to them. Experiment with gesture and tones of voice. Try your best to share and feel Shylock's angry demand for understanding. You'll end up face to face with your opponents, but keep your concentration! Repeat the exercise to give the first Solanio and Salarino a chance to read.

c Repeat Activity b, but this time Solanio and Salarino can reply. They should intercut the speech with insults to Shylock taken from this scene or other parts of the script (see the list on p. 188).

d 'The villainy you teach me I will execute' (line 56). Many critics believe this is the moment when Shylock decides on his revenge. What do you think?

e The speech contains ten rhetorical questions (exclamations phrased as questions to create dramatic effect rather than to seek an answer). Identify them and talk together about the effect created. Which do you think are the three most powerful and emotive ones?

---

jet semi-precious black stone
Rhenish fine white wine
prodigal waster
upon the mart into the marketplace
He was wont he liked
usurer money-lender

forfeit breaks the contract
hindered me stopped me making
what is his humility? how does he take it?
execute commit

SALARINO There is more difference between thy flesh and hers than between jet and ivory; more between your bloods than there is between red wine and Rhenish. But tell us, do you hear whether Antonio have had any loss at sea or no?

SHYLOCK There I have another bad match: a bankrupt, a prodigal, 35 who dare scarce show his head on the Rialto, a beggar that was used to come so smug upon the mart. Let him look to his bond. He was wont to call me usurer; let him look to his bond. He was wont to lend money for a Christian courtesy; let him look to his bond.

SALARINO Why, I am sure if he forfeit thou wilt not take his flesh. 40 What's that good for?

SHYLOCK To bait fish withal; if it will feed nothing else, it will feed my revenge. He hath disgraced me, and hindered me half a million, laughed at my losses, mocked at my gains, scorned my nation, thwarted my bargains, cooled my friends, heated mine enemies – 45 and what's his reason? I am a Jew. Hath not a Jew eyes? Hath not a Jew hands, organs, dimensions, senses, affections, passions? Fed with the same food, hurt with the same weapons, subject to the same diseases, healed by the same means, warmed and cooled by the same winter and summer as a Christian is? If you prick us, do 50 we not bleed? If you tickle us, do we not laugh? If you poison us, do we not die? And if you wrong us, shall we not revenge? If we are like you in the rest, we will resemble you in that. If a Jew wrong a Christian, what is his humility? Revenge. If a Christian wrong a Jew, what should his sufferance be by Christian example? Why, 55 revenge! The villainy you teach me I will execute, and it shall go hard but I will better the instruction.

Enter a [SERVING]MAN *from Antonio*

SERVINGMAN Gentlemen, my master Antonio is at his house, and desires to speak with you both.

SALARINO We have been up and down to seek him. 60

Enter TUBAL

SOLANIO Here comes another of the tribe; a third cannot be matched, unless the devil himself turn Jew.

Exeunt [Salarino and Solanio with the Servingman]

SHYLOCK How now, Tubal, what news from Genoa? Hast thou found my daughter?

Shylock rages about the money and jewels Jessica has taken. He wishes her dead. Tubal reports the loss of another of Antonio's ships. Shylock tells him to hire an officer to arrest Antonio.

---

1 His daughter or his money? (in pairs)

In lines 66–76 Shylock laments his betrayal. But is it the loss of his daughter or his wealth which affects him more?

Share a reading of the speech, varying your pace and tone to bring out his real feelings.

How do you respond to the view that Shylock's anger against his daughter is inhumane, cruel and unnecessarily vindictive?

2 Tubal: speak the sub-text (in pairs)

Tubal is important because he can give the audience an idea of how Shylock is regarded in the Jewish community. Is he sympathetic, or does he enjoy Shylock's discomfort? Choose parts and read lines 77–98. At the end of each speech, the partner playing Tubal should also speak aloud the thoughts the character might have about giving his news and Shylock's differing reactions to it.

3 See-sawing emotions (in pairs)

Focus on all Shylock's lines on the page opposite. One person reads them aloud, the other says either 'pleasure' or 'pain' at the end of each sentence to indicate Shylock's feelings at that moment. Afterwards, talk together about the fluctuations of his mood.

4 Leah: Mrs Shylock? (in small groups)

Judging by what Shylock says in lines 95–6, Leah seems to have been of great importance to him. Perhaps she was his wife, and therefore Jessica's mother. What do you think? Also, talk together about the significance of Jessica having no mother figure in the play.

---

hearsed coffined
lights lands
four score eighty
at a sitting at one go
divers many
break go bankrupt

turquoise turquoise ring
wilderness unlimited number
undone in big trouble
bespeak employ
make what merchandise drive what
  bargain

TUBAL I often came where I did hear of her, but cannot find her. 65

SHYLOCK Why there, there, there, there! A diamond gone cost me two thousand ducats in Frankfurt! The curse never fell upon our nation till now, I never felt it till now. Two thousand ducats in that, and other precious, precious jewels! I would my daughter were dead at my foot, and the jewels in her ear: would she were 70 hearsed at my foot, and the ducats in her coffin. No news of them, why so? And I know not what's spent in the search. Why thou loss upon loss – the thief gone with so much, and so much to find the thief, and no satisfaction, no revenge, nor no ill luck stirring but what lights o'my shoulders, no sighs but o'my breathing, no tears 75 but o'my shedding!

TUBAL Yes, other men have ill luck too. Antonio as I heard in Genoa –

SHYLOCK What, what, what? Ill luck, ill luck?

TUBAL – hath an argosy cast away coming from Tripolis. 80

SHYLOCK I thank God, I thank God. Is it true, is it true?

TUBAL I spoke with some of the sailors that escaped the wreck.

SHYLOCK I thank thee, good Tubal: good news, good news! Ha, ha, heard in Genoa!

TUBAL Your daughter spent in Genoa, as I heard, one night four score 85 ducats.

SHYLOCK Thou stick'st a dagger in me; I shall never see my gold again. Four score ducats at a sitting! Four score ducats!

TUBAL There came divers of Antonio's creditors in my company to Venice that swear he cannot choose but break. 90

SHYLOCK I am very glad of it. I'll plague him, I'll torture him. I am glad of it.

TUBAL One of them showed me a ring that he had of your daughter for a monkey.

SHYLOCK Out upon her! Thou torturest me, Tubal: it was my tur- 95 quoise, I had it of Leah when I was a bachelor. I would not have given it for a wilderness of monkeys.

TUBAL But Antonio is certainly undone.

SHYLOCK Nay, that's true, that very true. Go, Tubal, fee me an officer, bespeak him a fortnight before. I will have the heart of him if he 100 forfeit, for were he out of Venice I can make what merchandise I will. Go, Tubal, and meet me at our synagogue, go, good Tubal, at our synagogue, Tubal.

Exeunt

Portia urges Bassanio to delay before choosing. She could tell him how to choose correctly, but she must not break her oath of secrecy.

---

1 Portia: the first sign of nerves? (in pairs)

After a scene of hate, a scene of love, one which is also exceptionally rich in imagery. (You will find more activities and information on imagery on pp. 180–2.)

This third casket scene reveals how very differently Portia treats Bassanio from her other suitors. Until this scene, Portia has appeared as a composed, confident, even arrogant young woman, but what she says to Bassanio in lines 1–24 lacks her usual assurance and self-control.

a Read the lines aloud, taking turns to share them between you in any way you feel appropriate. Afterwards, talk together about how an actor in this speech might bring out Portia's feelings for Bassanio. Is Portia's hesitant and ambiguous style how someone in love speaks?

b List the differences between the way she thinks about and treats Bassanio and her attitude towards her earlier suitors.

2 Should women keep quiet? (in small groups)

In line 8 Portia seems to be saying that a woman should keep her feelings of love to herself: she can think of them, but not express them, perhaps leaving the man to take the initiative. Talk about what this remark adds to your understanding of how women are expected to behave in Venice and Belmont. In your discussion, also consider whether opinions like this are still expressed today, and how you feel about such views.

---

trains attendants
tarry wait
forbear be patient
but it . . . love I'm not saying I love you
Hate . . . quality hate doesn't make you feel like that
And yet . . . thought girls must keep their feelings to themselves

I am forsworn I've broken a promise
Beshrew curse (playfully)
naughty bad (naughty had a much stronger meaning in Shakespeare's time)
peize slow down
eche add to
election choosing

Act 3 Scene 2
Belmont   The great hall of Portia's house

Enter BASSANIO, PORTIA, GRATIANO, NERISSA, and all their trains

PORTIA I pray you tarry, pause a day or two
    Before you hazard, for in choosing wrong
    I lose your company; therefore forbear a while.
    There's something tells me, but it is not love,
    I would not lose you; and you know yourself   5
    Hate counsels not in such a quality.
    But lest you should not understand me well –
    And yet a maiden hath no tongue but thought –
    I would detain you here some month or two
    Before you venture for me. I could teach you   10
    How to choose right, but then I am forsworn.
    So will I never be. So may you miss me;
    But if you do, you'll make me wish a sin,
    That I had been forsworn. Beshrew your eyes!
    They have o'erlooked me and divided me: 15
    One half of me is yours, the other half yours –
    Mine own, I would say: but if mine then yours,
    And so all yours. O these naughty times
    Puts bars between the owners and their rights!
    And so though yours, not yours. Prove it so,   20
    Let Fortune go to hell for it, not I.
    I speak too long, but 'tis to peize the time,
    To eche it, and to draw it out in length,
    To stay you from election.

Bassanio is impatient to choose. He and Portia talk playfully of the treachery of love. He insists on choosing without delay. Portia, calling for music, compares him to a dying swan if defeated, and to Hercules should he succeed.

1 Impatience – and treachery?

a **Bassanio can't wait!** In lines 24–5 Bassanio is growing impatient and wants to get on with choosing. Think about what was going through his mind while he was listening to Portia, and write down his flow of thought.

b **The treachery of love?** An image of the rack runs through lines 24–38. The rack was an instrument of torture that stretched its victims' limbs. It was often used on traitors to make them confess to treason. Does Portia's interest in the word mean that she is suspicious of Bassanio's love? Are there other words or ideas that might challenge the integrity of Bassanio's intent? Read the lines carefully and decide what you think.

2 Music and mood

Portia calls for music to accompany Bassanio's choice. She also speaks in elaborate musical images. Select words and phrases from lines 40–62 which set the mood for Bassanio's big decision. What kind of musical comparisons does Portia make?

3 Portia as victim? Or . . .? (in pairs)

Portia recalls the story of how Hercules (Alcides) rescued the city of Troy from a sea monster which demanded that young girls be sacrificed to it (lines 54–62). She compares herself with these unfortunate young women, as if she were some sort of helpless victim. Talk together about whether or not you agree with Portia's view of herself. Is she serious or is she joking? Or what else might be going on?

---

amity friendship
enforcèd tortured
deliverance being released
aloof away
my eye . . . stream I'll cry a river
flourish fanfare

dulcet sweet
Alcides Hercules
Dardanian wives women of Troy
b.learèd visages tear-stained faces
The issue of th'exploit the outcome of Hercules' fight
fray battle or fight

BASSANIO   Let me choose,
     For as I am, I live upon the rack.   25
PORTIA Upon the rack, Bassanio? Then confess
     What treason there is mingled with your love.
BASSANIO None but that ugly treason of mistrust
     Which makes me fear th'enjoying of my love.
     There may as well be amity and life   30
     'Tween snow and fire, as treason and my love.
PORTIA Ay, but I fear you speak upon the rack
     Where men enforcèd do speak anything.
BASSANIO Promise me life and I'll confess the truth.
PORTIA Well then, confess and live.
BASSANIO   'Confess and love'   35
     Had been the very sum of my confession.
     O happy torment, when my torturer
     Doth teach me answers for deliverance!
     But let me to my fortune and the caskets.
PORTIA Away then! I am locked in one of them: 40
     If you do love me, you will find me out.
     Nerissa and the rest, stand all aloof,
     Let music sound while he doth make his choice;
     Then if he lose he makes a swan-like end,
     Fading in music. That the comparison   45
     May stand more proper, my eye shall be the stream
     And watery deathbed for him. He may win,
     And what is music then? Then music is
     Even as the flourish when true subjects bow
     To a new-crownèd monarch. Such it is   50
     As are those dulcet sounds in break of day,
     That creep into the dreaming bridegroom's ear
     And summon him to marriage. Now he goes
     With no less presence, but with much more love,
     Than young Alcides when he did redeem   55
     The virgin tribute paid by howling Troy
     To the sea-monster. I stand for sacrifice.
     The rest aloof are the Dardanian wives,
     With blearèd visages come forth to view
     The issue of th'exploit. Go, Hercules!   60
     Live thou, I live. With much much more dismay
     I view the fight than thou that mak'st the fray.

As music plays, Bassanio begins making his choice from the caskets. He considers false appearances in law, religion, war and beauty. In each case, vice can be concealed beneath a mask of virtue.

1 The casket song (in small groups)

a Bassanio's choosing is presented differently from the previous suitors'. A song (lines 63–72) accompanies his initial deliberations. Talk together about how you would stage this event. Who does the singing and what kind of music would you select? You might even set the words to your own music. Do you think the singer gives a rhyming hint to Bassanio about which casket to choose in 'bred', 'head', 'nourishèd'?

b The stage direction reads '*Bassanio comments on the caskets to himself*' during the song. What do you think is going through his mind?

2 Appearances are deceptive

Lines 73–101 express a major theme of the play: that appearance often does not match reality. People are frequently different from how they appear. Bassanio gives examples from a wide range of human experience. Speak the lines, pausing after each example. How many such images can you find?

fancy superficial love
begot created
ornament something which improves appearance
sober brow serious face
text quotation from a holy book

stayers stairs or ropes
valour's excrement a brave man's beard
redoubted feared
crispèd curly
wanton playful

[Here music.] A song the whilst Bassanio comments on the caskets
to himself

Tell me where is fancy bred,
Or in the heart, or in the head?
How begot, how nourishèd?   65
      Reply, reply.
It is engend'red in the eye,
With gazing fed, and fancy dies
In the cradle where it lies.
Let us all ring fancy's knell.   70
I'll begin it – Ding, dong, bell.

ALL   Ding, dong, bell.

BASSANIO So may the outward shows be least themselves:
The world is still deceived with ornament.
In law, what plea so tainted and corrupt   75
But, being seasoned with a gracious voice,
Obscures the show of evil? In religion,
What damnèd error but some sober brow
Will bless it and approve it with a text,
Hiding the grossness with fair ornament?   80
There is no vice so simple but assumes
Some mark of virtue on his outward parts.
How many cowards whose hearts are all as false
As stayers of sand, wear yet upon their chins
The beards of Hercules and frowning Mars,   85
Who inward searched have livers white as milk,
And these assume but valour's excrement
To render them redoubted. Look on beauty,
And you shall see 'tis purchased by the weight,
Which therein works a miracle in nature,   90
Making them lightest that wear most of it.
So are those crispèd snaky golden locks
Which maketh such wanton gambols with the wind
Upon supposèd fairness, often known
To be the dowry of a second head,   95
The skull that bred them in the sepulchre.

Bassanio rejects the gold and silver caskets because he fears that their fine appearance might be misleading. To Portia's delight, he chooses the lead casket. Inside he finds her portrait and a scroll.

1 Silver and gold (in pairs)

In lines 101–4 Bassanio has harsh words for gold and silver. In Greek mythology, everything King Midas touched, even his food, turned to gold. Silver is the servant of trade between men (but why not women?). Choose either gold or silver and represent Bassanio's words in a tableau, mime or drawing.

2 Bassanio's choice: the lead casket (in small groups)

Some people argue that Bassanio behaves out of character in choosing the lead casket because of his shady past and his motives for marrying Portia (see Act 1 Scene 1). Someone like that would more probably go for gold or silver! Talk about whether or not his choice is believable. Does it show that he is a genuine and sincere lover, not a fortune-hunter?

3 Portia's silence – does she know?

Portia's Aside (heard only by the audience) at lines 108–14 makes it clear that she is almost overwhelmed with passion and joy. Although Bassanio has yet to open the lead casket, she now knows that he has chosen correctly. How does this affect your view about Portia's role in the casket rituals?

4 Bassanio goes over the top – join him! (in pairs)

Lines 114–29 show Bassanio to be overjoyed to find Portia's portrait. He uses exaggerated, high-flown language (hyperbole or 'hype', see p. 180) to describe her. Read the speech aloud, using your partner as the subject. This activity has hilarious possibilities!

---

guilèd   treacherous
eloquence   fine appearance
fleet to air   disappear into thin air
allay   reduce
scant   ration
surfeit   have too much

sunder   keep apart
unfurnished   without a companion
substance   meaning
underprizing   not describing
  adequately
continent   contents

Thus ornament is but the guilèd shore
To a most dangerous sea; the beauteous scarf
Veiling an Indian beauty; in a word,
The seeming truth which cunning times put on   100
To entrap the wisest. Therefore thou gaudy gold,
Hard food for Midas, I will none of thee,
Nor none of thee, thou pale and common drudge
'Tween man and man. But thou, thou meagre lead
Which rather threaten'st than dost promise aught,   105
Thy paleness moves me more than eloquence:
And here choose I. Joy be the consequence!

PORTIA [*Aside*] How all the other passions fleet to air:
As doubtful thoughts, and rash-embraced despair,
And shudd'ring fear, and green-eyed jealousy!   110
O love, be moderate, allay thy ecstasy,
In measure rain thy joy, scant this excess!
I feel too much thy blessing: make it less
For fear I surfeit.
                    [*Bassanio opens the leaden casket*]

BASSANIO   What find I here?
Fair Portia's counterfeit! What demi-god   115
Hath come so near creation? Move these eyes?
Or whether riding on the balls of mine
Seem they in motion? Here are severed lips
Parted with sugar breath; so sweet a bar
Should sunder such sweet friends. Here in her hairs   120
The painter plays the spider, and hath woven
A golden mesh t'entrap the hearts of men
Faster than gnats in cobwebs. But her eyes –
How could he see to do them? Having made one,
Methinks it should have power to steal both his   125
And leave itself unfurnished. Yet look how far
The substance of my praise doth wrong this shadow
In underprizing it, so far this shadow
Doth limp behind the substance. Here's the scroll,
The continent and summary of my fortune.   130

The scroll confirms that Bassanio has won Portia. He asks her to approve the casket's truth. She wishes for his sake that she were a better and wealthier woman.

---

1 Make your version of the scroll

Shakespeare gives us the words that Bassanio reads, but what does the scroll actually look like? Produce your own version. Make it as authentic as possible.

2 Bassanio still can't believe his eyes (in pairs)

Bassanio has chosen correctly, confirming that success goes to the person who is not deceived by outward appearance. But he won't believe his good fortune until he has settled his engagement to Portia. Take turns to read aloud Bassanio's lines 139–48. How does line 148, with its echoes of commercialism and business practice, change the tone of what goes before?

3 Wealth – and absolute submission (in small groups)

a Share a group reading of lines 149–59 ('You see me . . . unpractised'). Portia begins by giving a very modest impression of herself, but increasingly includes words connected with wealth and value in her speech. As you read, draw attention to such words, then talk about the effect created.

b In lines 160–5 her commitment to Bassanio is absolute. Bassanio will be 'her lord, her governor, her king' (line 165). Is she wise to talk about herself in this way at the start of her life-long relationship with Bassanio? Give your response to that question; then, on a large sheet of paper, draw up a list of 'do's' and 'don'ts' for Portia at this vital time in her life.

---

by note as instructed
peals loud sounds
ratified approved

livings possessions, wealth
in gross in full

[He reads]
   'You that choose not by the view
   Chance as fair, and choose as true.
   Since this fortune falls to you,
   Be content and seek no new.
   If you be well pleased with this,   135
   And hold your fortune for your bliss,
   Turn you where your lady is,
   And claim her with a loving kiss.'
A gentle scroll! Fair lady, by your leave,
I come by note to give, and to receive.   140
Like one of two contending in a prize
That thinks he hath done well in people's eyes,
Hearing applause and universal shout,
Giddy in spirit, still gazing in a doubt
Whether those peals of praise be his or no –   145
So, thrice-fair lady, stand I even so,
As doubtful whether what I see be true,
Until confirmed, signed, ratified by you.

PORTIA You see me, Lord Bassanio, where I stand,
Such as I am. Though for myself alone   150
I would not be ambitious in my wish
To wish myself much better, yet for you
I would be trebled twenty times myself,
A thousand times more fair, ten thousand times
More rich, that only to stand high in your account   155
I might in virtues, beauties, livings, friends,
Exceed account. But the full sum of me
Is sum of something: which to term in gross
Is an unlessoned girl, unschooled, unpractised;
Happy in this, she is not yet so old   160
But she may learn; happier than this,
She is not bred so dull but she can learn;
Happiest of all, is that her gentle spirit
Commits itself to yours to be directed
As from her lord, her governor, her king.   165

Portia gives herself and all her wealth to Bassanio. She hands him a ring, saying its loss will mark the end of his love. Bassanio swears to wear it until his dying day. Gratiano asks for permission to marry Nerissa.

1 Question Portia (whole class)

Following Portia's complete submission to Bassanio (see Activity 3 on p. 88), now she quite literally gives herself to him (lines 166–7). What is your reaction to her attitude to her future husband? Each person makes a list of questions to ask Portia about her relationship with Bassanio. One volunteer takes the role of Portia to be questioned ('hot-seated') by the class. If Portia finds a question too difficult, she should say 'Time out', and possible answers can be discussed by everyone.

2 'With this ring . . .'

As was Elizabethan custom, Portia gives Bassanio a ring as a sign of her submission to him. Design an appropriate symbol or engraving for the ring. Perhaps use some of Portia's words from lines 166–74 as an inscription. (You will find the ring causes trouble later!)

3 Love at first sight (in pairs)

a Gratiano's line 198 speaks of his attraction for Nerissa, and celebrates the idea of love at first sight. Suggest why you think Shakespeare chose to follow Bassanio and Portia's betrothal with that of Gratiano and Nerissa. What effect does this have on the mood of the scene at this point?

b Gratiano and Nerissa's wedding plans depended on the outcome of Bassanio's choosing between the caskets. As Gratiano or Nerissa, write your account of the scene up to this point. You've had to listen to a great deal of talking while waiting for Bassanio's decision!

---

presage give warning of, foretell
vantage . . . you opportunity to show you up
bereft deprived
oration speech
wild of nothing loud hubbub

our . . . prosper our dreams come true
solemnise . . . faith get married
for intermission . . . than you I found a wife as quickly as you
as . . . falls by chance

Myself, and what is mine, to you and yours
Is now converted. But now I was the lord
Of this fair mansion, master of my servants,
Queen o'er myself; and even now, but now,
This house, these servants, and this same myself   170
Are yours, my lord's. I give them with this ring,
Which when you part from, lose, or give away,
Let it presage the ruin of your love,
And be my vantage to exclaim on you.

BASSANIO Madam, you have bereft me of all words.   175
Only my blood speaks to you in my veins,
And there is such confusion in my powers
As after some oration fairly spoke
By a belovèd prince there doth appear
Among the buzzing, pleasèd multitude,   180
Where every something being blent together
Turns to a wild of nothing, save of joy
Expressed, and not expressed. But when this ring
Parts from this finger, then parts life from hence:
O then be bold to say Bassanio's dead!   185

NERISSA My lord and lady, it is now our time,
That have stood by and seen our wishes prosper,
To cry 'good joy'. Good joy, my lord and lady!

GRATIANO My lord Bassanio, and my gentle lady,
I wish you all the joy that you can wish;   190
For I am sure you can wish none from me.
And when your honours mean to solemnise
The bargain of your faith, I do beseech you
Even at that time I may be married too.

BASSANIO With all my heart, so thou canst get a wife.   195

GRATIANO I thank your lordship, you have got me one.
My eyes, my lord, can look as swift as yours:
You saw the mistress, I beheld the maid.
You loved, I loved; for intermission
No more pertains to me, my lord, than you.   200
Your fortune stood upon the caskets there,
And so did mine too as the matter falls.

Gratiano gives an account of wooing Nerissa. Lorenzo, Jessica and Salerio arrive, having met on the way to Belmont.

---

1 What did Nerissa say? (in pairs)

It seems that Gratiano had a hard time courting Nerissa (lines 203–8). However, it is only he who gives details of the engagement; Nerissa is hardly given a chance to speak! What would she say about the affair?

Improvise a later conversation between Nerissa and Portia in which Nerissa explains how she was won over by Gratiano.

2 Gratiano wants a son (in pairs)

Gratiano may be joking about his proposed bet with Bassanio and Portia (lines 213–14) concerning which couple will produce the first son, but it shows that he values sons more than daughters. Talk together about reasons he might have for this attitude.

3 Jessica is un-named – is she welcome? (in small groups)

Line 217 is the only 'welcome' to Jessica on her arrival. She arrives at Belmont expecting to convert to Christianity, yet she is greeted as Lorenzo's 'infidel' and, like her father, denied the respect of a name. Bassanio welcomes Lorenzo and Salerio personally. Talk together about possible reasons for Portia and Bassanio apparently ignoring Jessica (in some productions, Jessica is coldly shunned upon her arrival).

4 Bassanio quickly feels at home

Only a few lines earlier, Bassanio's security depended on the lottery of the caskets. As he welcomes his guests at line 219, he has fully assumed his position as master of Belmont. What do you think about the ease with which he manages his sudden rise to power?

---

my very roof   the roof of my mouth
We'll play . . . ducats   we'll bet them a thousand ducats that we have the first son
stake down   lay a bet
infidel   non-Christian

If . . . welcome   If I'm not too new in my job here to greet you
entreat   beg
Commends . . . you   sends you his regards
estate   situation

For wooing here until I sweat again,
And swearing till my very roof was dry
With oaths of love, at last – if promise last –   205
I got a promise of this fair one here
To have her love, provided that your fortune
Achieved her mistress.

PORTIA   Is this true, Nerissa?

NERISSA Madam, it is, so you stand pleased withal.

BASSANIO And do you, Gratiano, mean good faith?   210

GRATIANO Yes 'faith, my lord.

BASSANIO Our feast shall be much honoured in your marriage.

GRATIANO We'll play with them the first boy for a thousand
    ducats.

NERISSA What, and stake down?   215

GRATIANO No, we shall ne'er win at that sport and stake down.
          But who comes here? Lorenzo and his infidel!
          What, and my old Venetian friend Salerio!

Enter LORENZO, JESSICA, *and* SALERIO, *a messenger from Venice*

BASSANIO Lorenzo and Salerio, welcome hither –
          If that the youth of my new interest here   220
          Have power to bid you welcome. By your leave
          I bid my very friends and countrymen,
          Sweet Portia, welcome.

PORTIA   So do I, my lord.
          They are entirely welcome.

LORENZO I thank your honour. For my part, my lord,   225
          My purpose was not to have seen you here,
          But meeting with Salerio by the way
          He did entreat me past all saying nay
          To come with him along.

SALERIO   I did, my lord,
          And I have reason for it. [*Giving letter*] Signor Antonio   230
          Commends him to you.

BASSANIO   Ere I ope his letter,
          I pray you tell me how my good friend doth.

SALERIO Not sick, my lord, unless it be in mind,
          Nor well, unless in mind: his letter there
          Will show you his estate.   235

Bassanio reads Antonio's letter, turning pale as he learns the bad news. He tells Portia of the debt he owes to Antonio, and asks Salerio to confirm the news of Antonio's shipwrecked vessels.

1 Antonio's letter: a prediction (in pairs)

Bassanio reads the letter from Antonio, but does not reveal exactly what it says until later in the scene. Use the clues on the page opposite to work out what the letter might say. Share your ideas, then read the actual letter (lines 314–19). Were you right?

2 'Nerissa, cheer yond stranger, bid her welcome' (in pairs)

Activity 3 on page 92 invited you to speculate about why Portia and Bassanio have no words of welcome for Jessica. Now Nerissa is instructed by Gratiano to welcome Jessica. Improvise the conversation between Nerissa and Jessica. Share it with the rest of the class.

In one production of the play, Nerissa was horrified by Gratiano's order. Talk together about the possible reasons for such a reaction from Nerissa.

3 'What, worse and worse?' (in groups of three or four)

There is a change of mood as Bassanio reads Antonio's bad news. The atmosphere of joy and triumph gives way to one of tension and concern.

First, read all the lines on the page opposite. Then, as a director, work out how you would show this change of mood to the audience.

Remember that you can rely on more than the language of the play. Think about the use of lighting and music. How might Gratiano, Salerio, Portia and Bassanio respond as the bad tidings from Venice sink in?

Jasons	see pages 10–11	**mere**	deadly
shrewd	unpleasant	**hit**	success
Rating	valuing	**'scape**	escape
braggart	boaster		

[Bassanio] opens the letter

GRATIANO Nerissa, cheer yond stranger, bid her welcome.
　　　　　Your hand, Salerio; what's the news from Venice?
　　　　　How doth that royal merchant, good Antonio?
　　　　　I know he will be glad of our success;
　　　　　We are the Jasons, we have won the fleece.　　　　240
SALERIO I would you had won the fleece that he hath lost.
PORTIA There are some shrewd contents in yond same paper
　　　　　That steals the colour from Bassanio's cheek:
　　　　　Some dear friend dead, else nothing in the world
　　　　　Could turn so much the constitution　　　　　245
　　　　　Of any constant man. What, worse and worse?
　　　　　With leave, Bassanio, I am half yourself
　　　　　And I must freely have the half of anything
　　　　　That this same paper brings you.
BASSANIO　　　　　　　　　　　　O sweet Portia,
　　　　　Here are a few of the unpleasant'st words　　　250
　　　　　That ever blotted paper. Gentle lady,
　　　　　When I did first impart my love to you,
　　　　　I freely told you all the wealth I had
　　　　　Ran in my veins: I was a gentleman.
　　　　　And then I told you true; and yet, dear lady,　　255
　　　　　Rating myself at nothing, you shall see
　　　　　How much I was a braggart. When I told you
　　　　　My state was nothing, I should then have told you
　　　　　That I was worse than nothing; for indeed
　　　　　I have engaged myself to a dear friend,　　　260
　　　　　Engaged my friend to his mere enemy,
　　　　　To feed my means. Here is a letter, lady,
　　　　　The paper as the body of my friend,
　　　　　And every word in it a gaping wound
　　　　　Issuing lifeblood. But is it true, Salerio?　　　265
　　　　　Hath all his ventures failed? What, not one hit?
　　　　　From Tripolis, from Mexico, and England,
　　　　　From Lisbon, Barbary, and India,
　　　　　And not one vessel 'scape the dreadful touch
　　　　　Of merchant-marring rocks?

Salerio confirms that all Antonio's ships are wrecked. He and Jessica tell of Shylock's burning desire to pursue the case against Antonio. Portia offers to cancel Antonio's debt and pay generous interest to Shylock.

1 'Twenty merchants, / The Duke himself, and the magnificoes' (whole class)

Salerio tells that all these people tried to persuade Shylock to release Antonio from his bond. As a whole class, reconstruct that scene. First, in small groups, discuss the questions and points these important people would raise with Shylock. Then, as a whole class, 'hot-seat' Shylock. Invent names for your character as merchant or magnifico. Your task is to persuade Shylock to cancel Antonio's bond.

2 Jessica – her tale – and her feelings

Jessica speaks only once (lines 283–9). She talks about her father and Antonio, confirming Salerio's typically Christian view that Shylock is inhuman, greedily pursuing Antonio's ruin.

a Write advice for the actress playing Jessica about how she should deliver this speech. Does she speak reluctantly, pressurised by the Christian characters around her into saying what they expect to hear? Or does she use this moment as a way of trying to get into their good books and align herself with the Christians?

b Jessica's elopement and marriage are never mentioned, Portia does not speak to her, and she listens in silence to Salerio's scornful words about her father. Write Jessica's diary entry, revealing her feelings on arriving at Belmont.

3 Portia: a woman who knows her own mind? (in pairs)

Portia's speech (lines 297–313) consists of eleven sentences. Seven of them are 'orders' and the others are emphatic statements. Read the lines to each other – first in a 'bossy' way, then in a different way. Talk together about what new aspects of her character they reveal.

---

discharge repay
plies plagues
impeach call in question

magnificoes / Of greatest port most important citizens
courtesies kind deeds
deface cancel

SALERIO   Not one, my lord.   270
    Besides, it should appear that if he had
    The present money to discharge the Jew,
    He would not take it. Never did I know
    A creature that did bear the shape of man
    So keen and greedy to confound a man.   275
    He plies the Duke at morning and at night,
    And doth impeach the freedom of the state
    If they deny him justice. Twenty merchants,
    The Duke himself, and the magnificoes
    Of greatest port have all persuaded with him,   280
    But none can drive him from the envious plea
    Of forfeiture, of justice, and his bond.
JESSICA When I was with him, I have heard him swear
    To Tubal and to Chus, his countrymen,
    That he would rather have Antonio's flesh   285
    Than twenty times the value of the sum
    That he did owe him; and I know, my lord,
    If law, authority, and power deny not
    It will go hard with poor Antonio.
PORTIA Is it your dear friend that is thus in trouble?   290
BASSANIO The dearest friend to me, the kindest man,
    The best conditioned and unwearied spirit
    In doing courtesies; and one in whom
    The ancient Roman honour more appears
    Than any that draws breath in Italy.   295
PORTIA What sums owes he the Jew?
BASSANIO For me, three thousand ducats.
PORTIA   What, no more?
    Pay him six thousand, and deface the bond.
    Double six thousand, and then treble that,
    Before a friend of this description   300
    Shall lose a hair through Bassanio's fault.
    First go with me to church, and call me wife,
    And then away to Venice to your friend!
    For never shall you lie by Portia's side
    With an unquiet soul. You shall have gold   305
    To pay the petty debt twenty times over.

Portia orders Bassanio to Venice to help Antonio. Bassanio reads Antonio's letter explaining his dreadful predicament. In Scene 3, Shylock orders the Jailer to guard Antonio closely.

1 'I will love you dear' (in pairs)

In line 312 Portia puns on the word 'dear'. This catches one of the main tensions of this scene (and the whole play): how far can money and love live comfortably together? Talk to each other about the relationship between Portia and Bassanio, and whether you think they really do love each other, or whether Bassanio still sees Portia as a 'lady richly left'.

2 Keeping Antonio in mind

As in Act 2 Scene 8, the audience does not see Antonio, but vivid impressions of him and his nature are given by other characters. Look back at the last three pages of script and make a note of all the references to Antonio. Use your list to write a paragraph on what the Christians think of him. Write another paragraph saying why the friendship between Antonio and Bassanio is so special.

3 Bassanio's letter

Imagine that Bassanio sends ahead of him a letter in response to Antonio's. Write Bassanio's letter.

4 What was the conversation about? (in groups of four)

Scene 3 begins with a conversation already in progress. The Jailer has probably been talking with Shylock before they enter. Improvise how the conversation started. According to Shylock, in line 1, someone mentioned 'mercy'! Remember there are four characters involved: Shylock, Solanio, Antonio and the Jailer. Involve them all in the conversation.

---

miscarried been wrecked
Nor rest . . . us twain I shall not sleep until we meet again

gratis free of interest
fond foolish or compassionate

When it is paid, bring your true friend along.
My maid Nerissa and myself meantime
Will live as maids and widows. Come away,
For you shall hence upon your wedding day.   310
Bid your friends welcome, show a merry cheer;
Since you are dear bought, I will love you dear.
But let me hear the letter of your friend.

BASSANIO [*Reads*] 'Sweet Bassanio, my ships have all miscarried, my
creditors grow cruel, my estate is very low; my bond to the Jew is   315
forfeit, and since in paying it, it is impossible I should live, all debts
are cleared between you and I if I might but see you at my death.
Notwithstanding, use your pleasure; if your love do not persuade
you to come, let not my letter.'

PORTIA O love! Dispatch all business and be gone.   320

BASSANIO Since I have your good leave to go away,
I will make haste. But till I come again
No bed shall e'er be guilty of my stay
Nor rest be interposer 'twixt us twain.

Exeunt

Act 3 Scene 3
Venice   A street

Enter SHYLOCK, SOLANIO, ANTONIO, and the Jailer

SHYLOCK Jailer, look to him. Tell not me of mercy.
This is the fool that lent out money gratis.
Jailer, look to him.

ANTONIO   Hear me yet, good Shylock –

SHYLOCK I'll have my bond, speak not against my bond;
I have sworn an oath that I will have my bond.   5
Thou call'dst me dog before thou hadst a cause,
But since I am a dog, beware my fangs.
The Duke shall grant me justice. I do wonder,
Thou naughty jailer, that thou art so fond
To come abroad with him at his request.   10

ANTONIO I pray thee hear me speak –

Antonio suspects that Shylock wants him dead because he has paid the debts of many of Shylock's clients. He feels that the Duke must uphold the law of Venice, and so is resigned to death.

1 Shylock: utterly implacable (in pairs)

In the short time he is on stage, Shylock dominates the dialogue – Antonio struggles to get a word in. Read the exchange aloud (lines 1– 17). Shylock should circle around Antonio, delivering each short sentence from a different angle to increase its power. Try it again with Shylock jabbing his finger sharply towards Antonio as he speaks. Work out how to bring out the menace of 'beware my fangs' and the insistent repetition of 'I'll have my bond'. Explore different ways of conveying Shylock's uncompromising, dominant mood.

2 Questioning Antonio (whole class)

You may already have 'hot-seated' Portia and Shylock. Now is your chance to question Antonio. Each person makes a list of points to ask Antonio. A volunteer Antonio can be told some questions in advance of the 'hot-seating'.

3 Thoughts from prison

Either imagine that you are Antonio, in your prison cell, the night before your trial. Shylock has the weight of the law on his side and you feel your death is inevitable. You can only hope that Bassanio will arrive in time 'to see [you] pay his debt'. Write down your thoughts in what you fear will be the last entry you will ever make in your diary.

Or give the Jailer a voice. He is one of Shakespeare's 'silent characters'. Write the entry he makes in the prison log book that evening. He is a man given to expressing his thoughts on his duties – so express them!

---

intercessors people who plead for others
bootless hopeless
forfeitures penalties (for breaking a contract)

commodity trade
impeach discredit
bated weakened

SHYLOCK I'll have my bond; I will not hear thee speak;
    I'll have my bond, and therefore speak no more.
    I'll not be made a soft and dull-eyed fool,
    To shake the head, relent, and sigh, and yield   15
    To Christian intercessors. Follow not!
    I'll have no speaking, I will have my bond.   *Exit*
SOLANIO It is the most impenetrable cur
    That ever kept with men.
ANTONIO   Let him alone.
    I'll follow him no more with bootless prayers.   20
    He seeks my life, his reason well I know:
    I oft delivered from his forfeitures
    Many that have at times made moan to me;
    Therefore he hates me.
SOLANIO   I am sure the Duke
    Will never grant this forfeiture to hold.   25
ANTONIO The Duke cannot deny the course of law;
    For the commodity that strangers have
    With us in Venice, if it be denied,
    Will much impeach the justice of the state,
    Since that the trade and profit of the city   30
    Consisteth of all nations. Therefore go.
    These griefs and losses have so bated me
    That I shall hardly spare a pound of flesh
    Tomorrow to my bloody creditor.
    Well, jailer, on. Pray God Bassanio come   35
    To see me pay his debt, and then I care not.
                         Exeunt

Lorenzo and Portia talk of the close friendship between Antonio and Bassanio. Portia says she plans to stay in a convent during Bassanio's absence. She appoints Lorenzo master of her household until her return.

1 Who's who? (in groups of four)

Stand in a circle. One person slowly reads Lorenzo's speech (lines 1–9). The others take the roles of Portia, Bassanio and Antonio. The whole group points at everyone mentioned on *every* mention; for example, there are three 'points' in line 1. (This pointing is called **deixis**. It sounds complicated, but is quickly mastered and will help your understanding of other passages in the play.)

2 Is Lorenzo a creep? (in groups of four)

Lorenzo's opening lines (1–4) praise Portia fulsomely. Talk together about the possible reasons why he is so excessive in his praise of Portia's qualities. Do you think he is being sincere, or is he overdoing the praise?

3 Friends resemble each other (in pairs)

The language of both characters in lines 1–21 is very formal and polite. Take parts and speak the lines. Don't worry if there are lines or phrases you don't understand (many people find the formality of the exchange creates difficulties). The general sense of the lines is: Lorenzo explains that if Portia knew what Antonio was truly like, she would be even prouder of her action in helping him. Portia replies (lines 11–18) that because close friends are always alike, Antonio must be like Bassanio in appearance, manner and spirit.

As at the end of the previous scene, the focus is on the intense friendship between Antonio and Bassanio. But do you agree with what Portia says? Talk together about whether close friends *are* like each other. Or do you choose your friends because they are unlike you?

---

conceit understanding
amity friendship
customary bounty habitual
 generosity or kindness
egal yoke equal sharing

lineaments appearance
bosom lover closest friend
husbandry and manage daily
 running of a household

Act 3 Scene 4
Belmont   A room in Portia's house

Enter PORTIA, NERISSA, LORENZO, JESSICA, and BALTHAZAR,
a man of Portia's

LORENZO Madam, although I speak it in your presence,
You have a noble and a true conceit
Of god-like amity, which appears most strongly
In bearing thus the absence of your lord.
But if you knew to whom you show this honour,   5
How true a gentleman you send relief,
How dear a lover of my lord your husband,
I know you would be prouder of the work
Than customary bounty can enforce you.

PORTIA I never did repent for doing good,   10
Nor shall not now; for in companions
That do converse and waste the time together,
Whose souls do bear an egal yoke of love,
There must be needs a like proportion
Of lineaments, of manners, and of spirit;   15
Which makes me think that this Antonio,
Being the bosom lover of my lord,
Must needs be like my lord. If it be so,
How little is the cost I have bestowed
In purchasing the semblance of my soul   20
From out the state of hellish cruelty!
This comes too near the praising of myself,
Therefore no more of it: hear other things.
Lorenzo, I commit into your hands
The husbandry and manage of my house   25
Until my lord's return; for mine own part
I have toward heaven breathed a secret vow
To live in prayer and contemplation,
Only attended by Nerissa here,
Until her husband and my lord's return.   30

Portia says she and Nerissa will stay at a convent. She sends her servant, Balthazar, to Padua to collect clothes and papers from Doctor Bellario.

---

1 Portia and Jessica – how do they relate? (in pairs)

Brief though it is, Jessica eventually manages to speak a line to Portia. Work on lines 42–4, reading the words aloud in different ways. Use gestures and movements to illustrate their relationship (or lack of one). In one modern production, Portia forgot Jessica's name at line 44 and had to be reminded of it. Try that version in your own explorations and discuss what point it makes about the relationship between the two women.

2 Jessica, standing in for Portia (in pairs)

Jessica will stand in for Portia as the mistress of Belmont while Portia is absent. As a Jew, she is now in charge of a Christian household and Portia has shown few signs of trusting or respecting her views. Improvise a scene where she shares her feelings about this responsibility with her husband Lorenzo.

3 Balthazar: the honest steward

Although he has been on stage from the beginning of this scene, nothing is known about Balthazar except that Portia has always found him 'honest-true'. Tell or write the story of the good deeds that Balthazar has previously done for Portia to win her trust.

4 The mystery letter: a prediction

Balthazar is to take a letter from Portia to Doctor Bellario in Padua. In reply, she expects 'notes and garments'. Before you turn the page, make predictions about what she is planning.

---

monastery convent   **traject** place for boarding the ferry
imposition duty

        There is a monastery two miles off,
        And there we will abide. I do desire you
        Not to deny this imposition,
        The which my love and some necessity
        Now lays upon you.
LORENZO   Madam, with all my heart   35
        I shall obey you in all fair commands.
PORTIA My people do already know my mind,
        And will acknowledge you and Jessica
        In place of Lord Bassanio and myself.
        So fare you well till we shall meet again.   40
LORENZO Fair thoughts and happy hours attend on you.
JESSICA I wish your ladyship all heart's content.
PORTIA I thank you for your wish, and am well pleased
        To wish it back on you: fare you well, Jessica.
                     Exeunt [Jessica and Lorenzo]
        Now, Balthazar –   45
        As I have ever found thee honest-true,
        So let me find thee still; take this same letter,
        And use thou all th'endeavour of a man
        In speed to Padua. See thou render this
        Into my cousin's hand, Doctor Bellario;   50
        And look, what notes and garments he doth give thee
        Bring them, I pray thee, with imagined speed
        Unto the traject, to the common ferry
        Which trades to Venice. Waste no time in words
        But get thee gone; I shall be there before thee.   55
BALTHAZAR Madam, I go with all convenient speed.   *[Exit]*
PORTIA Come on, Nerissa; I have work in hand
        That you yet know not of. We'll see our husbands
        Before they think of us.
NERISSA   Shall they see us?

Portia tells Nerissa of her plans. They will see their husbands again, but in disguise as men. In Scene 5, Lancelot fears that Jessica will be damned because she is a Jew's daughter.

1 What men are like (in pairs)

In lines 65–76, as Portia shares her plans to adopt a male disguise with Nerissa, she gives a range of images of typical male behaviour. Work on one or more of the following activities on the lines.

Either each choose one of these images and work out how to mime it for your partner to identify. Then work together on a single image that you will present to the rest of the class. Can the others recognise which image you chose?

Or write a short account of Portia's view of men as revealed in lines 65–76. Show how her words add to your understanding of Portia's attitudes.

Or make a list of five other habits or types of behaviour that the two women might adopt ('A thousand raw tricks . . . / Which I will practise') if they are going to convince other people of their 'manhood'. Your list may be serious or, like Portia's, mocking and satirical. Share your ideas with others in the class. Afterwards, try to rewrite your list in the same style and rhythm as lines 65–76.

2 Is Portia as innocent as she seems? (in pairs)

On two occasions Portia shows that she is fully alert to sexuality. Lines 61–2, 'accomplishèd / With that we lack', mean 'equipped with male genitals'. Then, in response to Nerissa's question (lines 79–80), she deliberately misunderstands the words 'turn to', interpreting them as 'sexually invite'. Talk together about what this adds to your understanding of Portia's character.

---

a habit clothes	**quaint** ingenious
accoutred dressed	**bragging jacks** boastful young men
'frays disputes, fights	**lewd** dirty-minded

PORTIA They shall, Nerissa, but in such a habit   60
        That they shall think we are accomplishèd
        With that we lack. I'll hold thee any wager,
        When we are both accoutred like young men
        I'll prove the prettier fellow of the two,
        And wear my dagger with the braver grace,   65
        And speak between the change of man and boy
        With a reed voice, and turn two mincing steps
        Into a manly stride; and speak of 'frays
        Like a fine bragging youth; and tell quaint lies
        How honourable ladies sought my love,   70
        Which I denying, they fell sick and died –
        I could not do withal. Then I'll repent,
        And wish for all that that I had not killed them;
        And twenty of these puny lies I'll tell,
        That men shall swear I have discontinued school   75
        Above a twelvemonth. I have within my mind
        A thousand raw tricks of these bragging jacks,
        Which I will practise.
NERISSA   Why, shall we turn to men?
PORTIA Fie, what a question's that,
        If thou wert near a lewd interpreter!   80
        But come, I'll tell thee all my whole device
        When I am in my coach, which stays for us
        At the park gate; and therefore haste away,
        For we must measure twenty miles today.

                                              Exeunt

Act 3 Scene 5
Belmont   Portia's garden

Enter LANCELOT the Clown and JESSICA

LANCELOT Yes truly, for look you, the sins of the father are to be laid
    upon the children. Therefore I promise you I fear you. I was
    always plain with you, and so now I speak my agitation of the
    matter. Therefore be o'good cheer, for truly I think you are
    damned. There is but one hope in it that can do you any good, and   5
    that is but a kind of bastard hope neither.

Jessica tells Lancelot that Lorenzo has converted her to Christianity. Lorenzo accuses Lancelot of making a black girl pregnant. Lancelot doesn't take it seriously.

---

1 Act out the scene (in groups of three)

Scene 5 is open to many interpretations. Prepare a performance or reading for the class. Keep in mind:

- how the conversation began
- what Lancelot and Jessica are doing in this particular place (are they working together, or is Lancelot waiting upon Jessica?)
- what feelings Lancelot and Jessica have for one another
- how serious Lancelot is in his taunting of Jessica, especially the implication that Jews are 'damned'
- whether Lorenzo really is jealous of Lancelot
- why Lancelot's relationship with 'the Moor' is mentioned now
- whether Lancelot hides his intelligence and feelings behind a mask of clowning
- the balance between seriousness and playfulness
- whether you wish the audience to feel deeply sympathetic towards these three characters at this moment.

You will find that the scene makes a fascinating human triangle. Use movement and gesture to enhance and increase the impact of your performance.

2 Lancelot and 'the Moor' (individually or in pairs)

It seems that Lancelot has made a black girl pregnant. Either as the girl (or as her father) write a letter to Bassanio complaining about his servant's irresponsible behaviour; or, act out the scene where the girl or her father goes to visit Bassanio.

Scylla a legendary sea monster
Charybdis a legendary whirlpool (the modern equivalent of Lancelot's dilemma is 'between the devil and the deep blue sea')

enow enough
e'en even
are out are arguing

JESSICA And what hope is that, I pray thee?

LANCELOT Marry, you may partly hope that your father got you not, that you are not the Jew's daughter.

JESSICA That were a kind of bastard hope indeed; so the sins of my 10
mother should be visited upon me.

LANCELOT Truly, then, I fear you are damned both by father and mother; thus when I shun Scylla your father, I fall into Charybdis your mother. Well, you are gone both ways.

JESSICA I shall be saved by my husband; he hath made me a Christian. 15

LANCELOT Truly, the more to blame he; we were Christians enow before, e'en as many as could well live one by another. This making of Christians will raise the price of hogs; if we grow all to be pork eaters, we shall not shortly have a rasher on the coals for money. 20

Enter LORENZO

JESSICA I'll tell my husband, Lancelot, what you say: here he comes.

LORENZO I shall grow jealous of you shortly, Lancelot, if you thus get my wife into corners.

JESSICA Nay, you need not fear us, Lorenzo: Lancelot and I are out. 25
He tells me flatly there's no mercy for me in heaven, because I am a Jew's daughter; and he says you are no good member of the commonwealth, for in converting Jews to Christians you raise the price of pork.

LORENZO I shall answer that better to the commonwealth than you can 30
the getting up of the Negro's belly: the Moor is with child by you, Lancelot.

LANCELOT It is much that the Moor should be more than reason; but if she be less than an honest woman, she is indeed more than I took her for. 35

LORENZO How every fool can play upon the word! I think the best grace of wit will shortly turn into silence, and discourse grow commendable in none only but parrots. Go in, sirrah, bid them prepare for dinner.

LANCELOT That is done, sir; they have all stomachs. 40

Lancelot deliberately misinterprets Lorenzo's words, but is sent off to arrange the serving of dinner. Jessica tells her husband how much she admires Portia. Lorenzo says he also has similar admirable qualities.

1 Prose and verse (in pairs)

After Lancelot's exit, Lorenzo and Jessica speak in verse, not prose. Talk together about why you think Shakespeare makes this change. Page 183 will help you.

2 Jessica: Portia's biggest fan? (in pairs)

Jessica appears to be a huge admirer of 'Lord Bassanio's wife'. Notice that Lorenzo does not use Portia's name now that she is married to his friend. Jessica's speech is full of glowing compliments about Portia, yet she may have little reason to like or respect her. Take turns to read lines 61–71 then talk together about:

- whether Portia deserves Jessica's praise
- why you think Jessica speaks of Portia in the language of religious adoration
- what image is created in lines 67–71 ('Pawned' means 'staked' or 'wagered'). Do you think the image is sexist? When you have talked about this, try drawing your version of the image!

3 But what does she think of Lorenzo? (in pairs)

As the two young lovers go in to dinner, Lorenzo comments that he is as admirable as Portia. Is he joking, or is he (as one production presented him) a humourless, pompous prig who treats his wife like a small child? Try both interpretations.

Jessica says that she will give her opinion of her husband later. Improvise the conversation that takes place over dinner when Jessica tells Lorenzo what she thinks of him.

---

cover   lay the table (but Lancelot pretends it means 'put your hat on')
humours and conceits   feelings and thoughts
O dear discretion ... suited!   what nit-picking, how he twists his words

planted   drawn up ready to fire
A many   how many
tricksy   ambiguous
Defy the matter   will not speak plainly
meet   fitting
rude   primitive

LORENZO Goodly Lord, what a witsnapper are you! Then bid them
    prepare dinner.

LANCELOT That is done too, sir; only 'cover' is the word.

LORENZO Will you cover then, sir?

LANCELOT Not so, sir, neither; I know my duty.   45

LORENZO Yet more quarrelling with occasion! Wilt thou show the
    whole wealth of thy wit in an instant? I pray thee understand a
    plain man in his plain meaning: go to thy fellows, bid them cover
    the table, serve in the meat, and we will come in to dinner.

LANCELOT For the table, sir, it shall be served in; for the meat, sir, it   50
    shall be covered; for your coming in to dinner, sir, why, let it be as
    humours and conceits shall govern.   *Exit*

LORENZO O dear discretion, how his words are suited!
          The fool hath planted in his memory
          An army of good words; and I do know   55
          A many fools that stand in better place,
          Garnished like him, that for a tricksy word
          Defy the matter. How cheer'st thou, Jessica?
          And now, good sweet, say thy opinion:
          How dost thou like the Lord Bassanio's wife?   60

JESSICA Past all expressing. It is very meet
          The Lord Bassanio live an upright life,
          For having such a blessing in his lady
          He finds the joys of heaven here on earth,
          And if on earth he do not merit it,   65
          In reason he should never come to heaven.
          Why, if two gods should play some heavenly match,
          And on the wager lay two earthly women,
          And Portia one, there must be something else
          Pawned with the other, for the poor rude world   70
          Hath not her fellow.

LORENZO   Even such a husband
          Hast thou of me, as she is for a wife.

JESSICA Nay, but ask my opinion too of that.

LORENZO I will anon; first let us go to dinner.

JESSICA Nay, let me praise you while I have a stomach.   75

LORENZO No, pray thee, let it serve for table talk;
          Then howsome'er thou speak'st, 'mong other things
          I shall digest it.

JESSICA   Well, I'll set you forth.

                                  Exeunt

Looking back at Act 3
Activities for groups or individuals

___

1 Scenes of love and hate

Hate and love alternate throughout Act 3. Take a large piece of sugar paper and draw a 'timeline' across it, running from Act 3 Scene 1 to Scene 5. Reread all the scenes and as you come across an example of hate, put it above the line; put examples of love below it. Display your findings and talk about the dramatic effects created by the patterning.

2 Venice and Belmont

What impressions of Belmont have you acquired so far in the play? Using the template below, complete ten contrasting sentences for the two locations, Venice and Belmont:

Belmont is _____; Venice is _____.

3 Design a 'Wanted' poster

In Scene 1 Shylock orders Antonio's arrest. Design the 'Wanted' poster which might be pasted up around Venice. Give details of Antonio's 'crime' and probable punishment. Remember: Shylock is likely to write the poster's contents himself.

4 Shylock's repetitions

In Scene 1 Shylock often repeats certain words and phrases. Make a full list of his repetitions. Decide why these words are of such importance to him. What is the dramatic effect of Shylock speaking in this way?

5 The most important lines?

> The villainy you teach me I will execute, and it shall go hard but I
> will better the instruction.   *Act 3 Scene 1, lines 56–7*

The director Sir Peter Hall described these lines as the most important in the play, because they show Shakespeare's understanding of why Shylock behaves so harshly. Talk together about whether you agree with this view.

6 Why does Shylock hate Antonio?

'I oft delivered from his forfeitures / Many that have at times made moan to me' (Act 3 Scene 3, lines 22–3) is Antonio's explanation for Shylock's hatred of him. Shylock probably has other reasons for his hatred. Make a full list of Shylock's reasons for hating Antonio. Give short quotations from the script as an example of each reason.

7 Tubal speaks out!

Tubal appears in only one scene (Act 3 Scene 1) and speaks twelve lines. Give him more of a voice! Look at the picture above (he has his back to the audience). What is in his mind as he listens to Shylock's anguish? Write his thoughts as an interior monologue.

The Duke's court assembles to judge Shylock's case against Antonio. The Duke sympathises with Antonio, and tells Shylock that he expects him to show mercy at the last moment.

1 Stage the entrances (in large groups)

Use the stage direction to allocate parts. Work out how to stage the Duke's entrance. Bear in mind that the magnificoes (high-ranking Venetians) would be his fellow judges. Where would they sit? Then stage Shylock's entrance, which in Shakespeare's time would have been from the left, the side associated with evil (the Latin word for 'on the left' is *sinister*). Think of the effect you would wish to create as Shylock is received in a court full of Christians. (You will find pictures of three different trial scenes on pages x and 193 to help you.)

2 Is the Duke biased? (in pairs)

Take turns to read the Duke's lines 3–6. Talk together about whether they suggest that the Duke will be fair and impartial in the case against Antonio.

3 Shylock answers back (in groups of three)

The Duke and Antonio both criticise Shylock in lines 3–13. Imagine that he has chance to answer back to the accusations they make. Take parts as the three characters. As the Duke and Antonio read, pause after each critical comment for Shylock to offer his side of things.

4 Shylock: what's he thinking?

Shylock is 'ready at the door' (line 15). Imagine that Shakespeare has written a soliloquy for him in which he reveals his true feelings to the audience. Write your own version of Shylock's soliloquy, expressing his feelings at this dramatic moment in the play. He is about to enter a room full of enemies, but might be only minutes from gaining his much desired revenge.

---

adversary opponent
dram drop
tane taken
obdùrate stubborn
envy hatred
thou . . . act you will keep up this pretence only until the last moment

remorse pity
loose cancel
Forgive . . . principal ask for repayment of only some of the loan
Enow enough

Act 4 Scene 1
The Duke's palace in Venice

Enter the DUKE, *the Magnificoes,* ANTONIO, BASSANIO, SALERIO, *and* GRATIANO, *with others*

DUKE What, is Antonio here?

ANTONIO Ready, so please your grace.

DUKE I am sorry for thee. Thou art come to answer
    A stony adversary, an inhuman wretch,
    Uncapable of pity, void and empty   5
    From any dram of mercy.

ANTONIO   I have heard
    Your grace hath tane great pains to qualify
    His rigorous course; but since he stands obdùrate
    And that no lawful means can carry me
    Out of his envy's reach, I do oppose   10
    My patience to his fury, and am armed
    To suffer with a quietness of spirit
    The very tyranny and rage of his.

DUKE Go one and call the Jew into the court.

SALERIO He is ready at the door; he comes, my lord.   15

Enter SHYLOCK

DUKE Make room and let him stand before our face.
    Shylock, the world thinks, and I think so too,
    That thou but leadest this fashion of thy malice
    To the last hour of act, and then 'tis thought
    Thou'lt show thy mercy and remorse more strange   20
    Than is thy strange apparent cruelty.
    And where thou now exacts the penalty,
    Which is a pound of this poor merchant's flesh,
    Thou wilt not only loose the forfeiture
    But, touched with human gentleness and love,   25
    Forgive a moiety of the principal,
    Glancing an eye of pity on his losses
    That have of late so huddled on his back,
    Enow to press a royal merchant down

The Duke asks Shylock to show pity. Shylock refuses to give his reasons for wishing to harm Antonio, except that it is his whim, and that he hates him.

---

1 The Duke's appeal to Shylock (in small groups)

Try a group reading of lines 16–34, sharing the lines between you. Look out for clues to the Duke's feelings for Antonio and his attitudes to non-Christians. After your reading, summarise the key points he makes in this opening address.

2 Shylock's opening statement (in pairs)

a **Shylock won't explain**   Take turns to read aloud lines 35–62, changing over at the end of each line or at each punctuation mark. Earlier in the play (Act 1 Scene 3, lines 34–43) Shylock expressed his grievances against Antonio; yet now, in the court, he refuses to discuss his feelings, except to confirm his hatred for Antonio (line 60). Talk together about the possible reasons for Shylock's behaviour at this vital point in his revenge plan.

b **Shylock's curse**   Shylock is determined to use the Venetian code of law to press his case against Antonio. If the Duke will not enforce the law, then 'the danger' will result (lines 38–9). Write a paragraph to show what you imagine Shylock wishes might happen to 'your charter and your city's freedom' if the law is not followed.

3 Bizarre fears (in pairs)

In lines 47–52 Shylock lists three extraordinary things which some men find disturbing or hateful. First, discuss why you think he uses such peculiar examples, then extend his list by inventing three more outlandish fears. Write them in the same style that Shylock uses.

And pluck . . . flint and make even the most hard-hearted feel sorry for him
Turks, and Tartars seen by Christians as heathens (like the Jews)
baned poisoned

affection . . . passion strong feelings often disturb the mind
but of . . . offended but can't help offending others because he himself is so offended

And pluck commiseration of his state   30
From brassy bosoms and rough hearts of flint,
From stubborn Turks, and Tartars never trained
To offices of tender courtesy.
We all expect a gentle answer, Jew.

SHYLOCK I have possessed your grace of what I purpose,   35
And by our holy Sabaoth have I sworn
To have the due and forfeit of my bond.
If you deny it, let the danger light
Upon your charter and your city's freedom!
You'll ask me why I rather choose to have   40
A weight of carrion flesh than to receive
Three thousand ducats. I'll not answer that –
But say it is my humour: is it answered?
What if my house be troubled with a rat,
And I be pleased to give ten thousand ducats   45
To have it baned? What, are you answered yet?
Some men there are love not a gaping pig;
Some that are mad if they behold a cat;
And others when the bagpipe sings i'the nose
Cannot contain their urine: for affection   50
Masters oft passion, sways it to the mood
Of what it likes or loathes. Now for your answer:
As there is no firm reason to be rendered
Why he cannot abide a gaping pig,
Why he a harmless necessary cat,   55
Why he a woollen bagpipe, but of force
Must yield to such inevitable shame
As to offend, himself being offended:
So can I give no reason, nor I will not,
More than a lodged hate and a certain loathing   60
I bear Antonio, that I follow thus
A losing suit against him. Are you answered?

BASSANIO This is no answer, thou unfeeling man,
To excuse the current of thy cruelty.

Antonio says it's pointless to argue with the pitiless Shylock. Bassanio's offer of six thousand ducats is refused. Shylock demands the pound of flesh as his property, and due to him by law.

---

1 Bassanio gets involved – a quick-fire exchange (in pairs)

Take parts as Bassanio and Shylock and read lines 63–9. Experiment with different ways of presenting the two men sparring verbally with each other.

2 Shylock: a force of nature (in pairs)

a In lines 70–83 Antonio stresses how immovable and stubborn Shylock is. Reasoning with him is like trying to arrest nature itself. It is impossible to stop the waves on the beach or the wolf eating the lamb, or the branches moving in the wind. Perhaps Shakespeare had the story of King Canute in his mind here (especially in lines 71–2). If you don't know the story, research it in the library or on the Internet. Write a paragraph explaining ways in which it mirrors Antonio's comparisons.

b Make up another futile task to add to Antonio's list. Mime it to the rest of the class. Can they tell what it is?

3 Give me judgement!

Lines 89–103 are Shylock's passionate plea for his case to be heard. Try one or more of the following:

a Learn and rehearse his speech for performance. Bring out Shylock's vehemence and commitment.

b Shylock speaks out about the abuse of slaves. Does this affect how you respond to him?

c Write several paragraphs about what Shylock's words tell you about master–slave relationships in Venice, and how that knowledge adds to your understanding of Venetian society.

d How does the Duke respond as he listens to Shylock's tirade against the masters of Venice? Taking each sentence in turn, write the Duke's unspoken thoughts on what he hears.

Every . . . first not all insults provoke hatred at first
bate reduce
fretten disturbed, blown about
moe more
brief and plain conveniency speed

rendering giving
palates mouths
viands food
fie upon so much for
decrees laws

SHYLOCK I am not bound to please thee with my answers.   65
BASSANIO Do all men kill the things they do not love?
SHYLOCK Hates any man the thing he would not kill?
BASSANIO Every offence is not a hate at first.
SHYLOCK What, wouldst thou have a serpent sting thee twice?
ANTONIO I pray you think you question with the Jew.   70
       You may as well go stand upon the beach
       And bid the main flood bate his usual height;
       You may as well use question with the wolf
       Why he hath made the ewe bleat for the lamb;
       You may as well forbid the mountain pines   75
       To wag their high tops and to make no noise
       When they are fretten with the gusts of heaven;
       You may as well do anything most hard
       As seek to soften that – than which what's harder? –
       His Jewish heart. Therefore I do beseech you   80
       Make no moe offers, use no farther means,
       But with all brief and plain conveniency
       Let me have judgement, and the Jew his will.
BASSANIO For thy three thousand ducats here is six.
SHYLOCK If every ducat in six thousand ducats   85
       Were in six parts, and every part a ducat,
       I would not draw them; I would have my bond.
DUKE How shalt thou hope for mercy, rendering none?
SHYLOCK What judgement shall I dread, doing no wrong?
       You have among you many a purchased slave,   90
       Which, like your asses and your dogs and mules,
       You use in abject and in slavish parts
       Because you bought them. Shall I say to you,
       'Let them be free! Marry them to your heirs!
       Why sweat they under burdens? Let their beds   95
       Be made as soft as yours, and let their palates
       Be seasoned with such viands'? You will answer,
       'The slaves are ours.' So do I answer you.
       The pound of flesh which I demand of him
       Is dearly bought; 'tis mine, and I will have it.   100
       If you deny me, fie upon your law:
       There is no force in the decrees of Venice.
       I stand for judgement. Answer: shall I have it?

Nerissa, disguised as a lawyer's clerk, arrives with letters from Bellario, a legal expert. Shylock sharpens his knife on the sole of his shoe, and Gratiano abuses him for his cruel nature.

1 Shylock sharpens his knife (in pairs)

Bassanio tries to cheer Antonio (lines 111–13), and offers to take Antonio's place as Shylock pursues his forfeit. But Antonio insists (lines 114–18) that he must be the one to die. Shylock seems to ignore the two men's evident affection for each other, and begins to sharpen his knife. Read the lines aloud, then talk together about your impressions of the two men and their bond to each other.

Which line do you think Shylock is speaking at this moment?

2 Gratiano attacks (in small groups)

Gratiano viciously abuses Shylock, saying that a dead wolf's soul entered his body whilst he was still in his mother's womb. One person, as Shylock, sits on a chair. The others speak, shout or sneer lines 128–38 at him, changing over at each punctuation mark. Take turns to be Shylock. Afterwards talk together about:

- how Shylock probably feels
- your understanding of 'Pythagoras' in this context (see gloss below)
- what these lines suggest about Gratiano.

determine settle	**keen** sharp (or sing a funeral song)
stays without waits outside	**wit** intelligence
Ere before	**inexecrable** utterly cursed
tainted wether sick ram	**Pythagoras** Greek who taught the
Meetest the most suitable	idea of the transmigration of souls
epitaph words on a tomb or	**trunks** bodies
gravestone	**unhallowed dam** heathen mother

DUKE Upon my power I may dismiss this court,
        Unless Bellario, a learned doctor   105
        Whom I have sent for to determine this,
        Come here today.
SALERIO   My lord, here stays without
        A messenger with letters from the doctor,
        New come from Padua.
DUKE Bring us the letters. Call the messenger.   110
BASSANIO Good cheer, Antonio! What, man, courage yet!
        The Jew shall have my flesh, blood, bones, and all,
        Ere thou shalt lose for me one drop of blood.
ANTONIO I am a tainted wether of the flock,
        Meetest for death; the weakest kind of fruit   115
        Drops earliest to the ground, and so let me.
        You cannot better be employed, Bassanio,
        Than to live still and write mine epitaph.

      Enter NERISSA [*disguised as a lawyer's clerk*]

DUKE Came you from Padua, from Bellario?
NERISSA From both, my lord: [*Presenting letter*] Bellario greets your
        grace.   120
BASSANIO Why dost thou whet thy knife so earnestly?
SHYLOCK To cut the forfeiture from that bankrupt there.
GRATIANO Not on thy sole, but on thy soul, harsh Jew,
        Thou mak'st thy knife keen. But no metal can,
        No, not the hangman's axe, bear half the keenness   125
        Of thy sharp envy. Can no prayers pierce thee?
SHYLOCK No, none that thou hast wit enough to make.
GRATIANO O be thou damned, inexecrable dog,
        And for thy life let justice be accused!
        Thou almost mak'st me waver in my faith,   130
        To hold opinion with Pythagoras
        That souls of animals infuse themselves
        Into the trunks of men. Thy currish spirit
        Governed a wolf, who – hanged for human slaughter –
        Even from the gallows did his fell soul fleet,   135
        And whilst thou layest in thy unhallowed dam
        Infused itself in thee; for thy desires
        Are wolfish, bloody, starved, and ravenous.

Bellario's letter is read out. He is ill, but has sent Doctor Balthazar in his place. Portia enters in disguise as Balthazar and announces that she is fully informed of the case.

---

1 The Duke's letter to Bellario

We learn from Bellario (line 150) that the Duke had contacted him by letter to request his assistance with this difficult and embarrassing case. Write your version of the Duke's letter.

2 Bellario's letter (in groups of six)

a **Point out who's involved**   Take a part each (Bellario, Balthazar, Antonio, Shylock, the Duke, the Duke's messenger). Stand in a circle. Bellario reads the letter, slowly. Everyone points to whoever is mentioned in any way (e.g. 'Your grace', 'I', 'your'). Afterwards, talk together about how this activity helps your understanding. (See also Activity 1, p. 102.)

b **Balthazar: a legal whiz-kid**   The letter is part of Portia's disguise. It pays 'Balthazar' many compliments. Pick out the words and phrases about him which are intended to impress the court. Pool your suggestions about why Portia wants these to be heard before she enters the courtroom.

3 The trial begins (in groups of six)

The long, famous trial scene runs from line 165 to line 396. The best thing to do is to get a feeling for the whole episode and how Shakespeare builds up the dramatic tension. So, take parts as Portia, the Duke, Shylock, Antonio, Bassanio and Gratiano and read straight through without pause. Afterwards, work on some of the activities on pages 124–36.

---

rail   abuse, revile
wit   intelligence
loving visitation   friendly visit
furnished   provided
importunity   pressing request
stead   place

I beseech . . . estimation   Take my advice: don't let his youth stop you from respecting him
whose . . . commendation   the trial will improve his reputation
difference   dispute

SHYLOCK Till thou canst rail the seal from off my bond
      Thou but offend'st thy lungs to speak so loud.   140
      Repair thy wit, good youth, or it will fall
      To cureless ruin. I stand here for law.
DUKE This letter from Bellario doth commend
      A young and learned doctor to our court:
      Where is he?
NERISSA   He attendeth here hard by   145
      To know your answer whether you'll admit him.
DUKE With all my heart. Some three or four of you
      Go give him courteous conduct to this place.
                               [*Exeunt officials*]
      Meantime the court shall hear Bellario's letter.
[*Reads*] 'Your grace shall understand, that at the receipt of your letter   150
I am very sick; but in the instant that your messenger came, in
loving visitation was with me a young doctor of Rome: his name
is Balthazar. I acquainted him with the cause in controversy
between the Jew and Antonio the merchant. We turned o'er many
books together; he is furnished with my opinion which, bettered   155
with his own learning, the greatness whereof I cannot enough
commend, comes with him at my importunity, to fill up your
grace's request in my stead. I beseech you let his lack of years be
no impediment to let him lack a reverend estimation, for I never
knew so young a body with so old a head. I leave him to your   160
gracious acceptance, whose trial shall better publish his commendation.'

Enter PORTIA [*disguised as Doctor Balthazar, followed by officials*]

      You hear the learn'd Bellario what he writes,
      And here I take it is the doctor come.
      Give me your hand. Come you from old Bellario?   165
PORTIA I did, my lord.
DUKE   You are welcome; take your place.
      Are you acquainted with the difference
      That holds this present question in the court?
PORTIA I am informèd throughly of the cause.
      Which is the merchant here and which the Jew?   170

Portia appeals unsuccessfully to Shylock to show mercy. She explains that mercy can be neither forced nor diluted, and is greater than any monarch's power. Mercy and justice should go hand in hand, for mercy, not justice, will save us.

---

1 'The quality of mercy' (in small groups)

Portia's speech is world-famous. Try some of the following activities to help you understand its powerful appeal to women and men in all ages and all cultures.

a Stand in a circle. Take turns to read aloud lines 180–93, handing over at each punctuation mark. Now read them again, but this time each reader adds a mime to illustrate the language. The whole group should then repeat the reader's words and actions.

b Discuss whether, in line 193, Portia is openly anti-Semitic when she addresses Shylock as 'Jew'. Might he also be offended by her reference to 'gentle' (line 181) which puns on the word 'gentile' (a non-Jew; see p. 54)?

c Look back to Shylock's speech (Act 3 Scene 1, lines 42–57) in which he declared not only his desire for revenge but also his common humanity with other men. Talk about the ways in which Portia's lines counterbalance Shylock's declamation. Present your response to the rest of the class in a dramatic or visual way.

d Organise your own class debate about the conflict between justice and mercy. Should those who were guilty of the Holocaust have been shown mercy or justice? Would you follow Portia's advice and show mercy as well as justice to the Nazi soldier in this photograph?

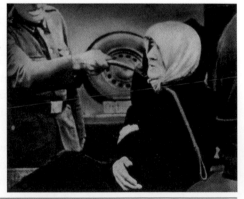

---

impugn oppose	**seasons** blends with
becomes suits	**salvation** life after death in heaven
temporal earthly	**render . . . mercy** behave mercifully
attribute to quality of	**mitigate** moderate or tone down
sceptred sway authority of a monarch	

DUKE Antonio and old Shylock, both stand forth.
PORTIA Is your name Shylock?
SHYLOCK   Shylock is my name.
PORTIA Of a strange nature is the suit you follow,
          Yet in such rule that the Venetian law
          Cannot impugn you as you do proceed.   175
          – You stand within his danger, do you not?
ANTONIO Ay, so he says.
PORTIA   Do you confess the bond?
ANTONIO I do.
PORTIA   Then must the Jew be merciful.
SHYLOCK On what compulsion must I? Tell me that.
PORTIA The quality of mercy is not strained,   180
          It droppeth as the gentle rain from heaven
          Upon the place beneath. It is twice blest:
          It blesseth him that gives, and him that takes.
          'Tis mightiest in the mightiest, it becomes
          The thronèd monarch better than his crown.   185
          His sceptre shows the force of temporal power,
          The attribute to awe and majesty,
          Wherein doth sit the dread and fear of kings;
          But mercy is above this sceptred sway.
          It is enthronèd in the hearts of kings,   190
          It is an attribute to God himself,
          And earthly power doth then show likest God's
          When mercy seasons justice. Therefore, Jew,
          Though justice be thy plea, consider this:
          That in the course of justice, none of us   195
          Should see salvation. We do pray for mercy,
          And that same prayer doth teach us all to render
          The deeds of mercy. I have spoke thus much
          To mitigate the justice of thy plea,
          Which if thou follow, this strict court of Venice   200
          Must needs give sentence 'gainst the merchant there.

Bassanio asks Portia to bend the law to save Antonio, but she refuses, as other legal cases would be affected. Despite offers of trebled payment, Shylock implacably refuses to give way.

1 Doesn't her husband recognise her? (in pairs)

Portia and Bassanio have a conversation, yet he does not see through her disguise. In Shakespeare's time such disguises were accepted without question. Work together on their exchange and decide how Portia's appearance, tone of voice and movement can make Bassanio's lack of recognition seem credible.

2 The end justifies the means? (in small groups)

'To do a great right, do a little wrong', says Bassanio (line 212). Has he got a point? Would you do wrong if you thought it would result in good? Discuss this, giving examples.

3 Appearance versus reality (in pairs)

a The theme of appearance comes over strongly as Shylock more and more believes that Portia/Balthazar supports him. Read lines 219–52, noting how Shylock praises Balthazar. Then prepare two tableaux: the first showing Shylock's opinion of Portia, the second revealing her true attitude. After your tableaux, talk together about how Portia's deception of Shylock might affect the audience's response to him.

b Antonio is similarly deceived by Portia's performance. The pressure he feels under emerges in lines 239–40. Talk together about his possible changing reactions to all that is said opposite. Suggest how his thoughts culminate in his urgent plea for a quick decision.

My deeds . . . head! I'll take responsibility for my own actions
crave demand
malice evil
Wrest . . . authority use your power to change the law
curb deprive
'Twill . . . state many other cases will be mistakenly based on this one as a precedent

precedent a case to be used as an example
Daniel Jewish prophet known for revealing the truth and promoting justice
perjury lying under oath
tenour small print
exposition explanation

SHYLOCK My deeds upon my head! I crave the law,
   The penalty and forfeit of my bond.
PORTIA Is he not able to discharge the money?
BASSANIO Yes, here I tender it for him in the court,   205
   Yea, twice the sum; if that will not suffice,
   I will be bound to pay it ten times o'er
   On forfeit of my hands, my head, my heart.
   If this will not suffice, it must appear
   That malice bears down truth. And I beseech you   210
   Wrest once the law to your authority;
   To do a great right, do a little wrong,
   And curb this cruel devil of his will.
PORTIA It must not be; there is no power in Venice
   Can alter a decree establishèd.   215
   'Twill be recorded for a precedent,
   And many an error by the same example
   Will rush into the state: it cannot be.
SHYLOCK A Daniel come to judgement; yea a Daniel!
   O wise young judge, how I do honour thee!   220
PORTIA I pray you let me look upon the bond.
SHYLOCK Here 'tis, most reverend doctor, here it is.
PORTIA Shylock, there's thrice thy money offered thee.
SHYLOCK An oath, an oath. I have an oath in heaven!
   Shall I lay perjury upon my soul?   225
   No, not for Venice.
PORTIA   Why, this bond is forfeit,
   And lawfully by this the Jew may claim
   A pound of flesh, to be by him cut off
   Nearest the merchant's heart. Be merciful:
   Take thrice thy money; bid me tear the bond.   230
SHYLOCK When it is paid, according to the tenour.
   It doth appear you are a worthy judge,
   You know the law, your exposition
   Hath been most sound. I charge you by the law,
   Whereof you are a well-deserving pillar,   235
   Proceed to judgement. By my soul I swear
   There is no power in the tongue of man
   To alter me. I stay here on my bond.
ANTONIO Most heartily I do beseech the court
   To give the judgement.

Portia judges that Shylock must have his pound of flesh. Antonio is now prepared to die. He lovingly bids farewell to Bassanio, saying that he is glad to be spared a life of poverty.

1 A game of cat and mouse (in pairs)

a **Racking up the tension**   Take parts and read lines 240–58. Shakespeare allows Shylock and Portia to share lines and trade ideas quickly so that the pace and tension mount. Practise ways of showing the gathering excitement.

b **Add the stage directions**   There are no stage directions for this page, but it is clear from the script that a great deal is happening. Make a list (with line numbers) of the movements and gestures you would direct actors to use in lines 240–60.

2 'Some surgeon' – is it in the bond?

Shylock sticks to the letter of the bond as he refuses to supply a surgeon to stop Antonio's wounds. As a bystander in the court, write a paragraph giving your reactions to the exchange about the surgeon in lines 253–8.

3 Antonio's farewell (in pairs)

Antonio's farewell to Bassanio can be a profoundly moving moment in performance. Work together on how the two actors might handle lines 260–77 to affect the audience's emotions. Experiment with different versions of how Antonio speaks and moves, and how Bassanio reacts. Take into account:

- that Antonio expresses gratitude to 'Fortune' for granting him death, rather than poverty
- the dramatic irony as Antonio speaks of Bassanio's wife. Neither man realises she hears everything.

---

intent and purpose   meaning and intention
Hath . . . to   fully authorise
balance   scales
armed   ready
Fortune   fate

is her custom   usual
use   habit
speak . . . death   speak well of me when I'm gone
Repent but you   just feel sorry

PORTIA   Why then, thus it is: 240
    You must prepare your bosom for his knife.
SHYLOCK O noble judge, O excellent young man!
PORTIA For the intent and purpose of the law
    Hath full relation to the penalty
    Which here appeareth due upon the bond.   245
SHYLOCK 'Tis very true. O wise and upright judge,
    How much more elder art thou than thy looks!
PORTIA Therefore lay bare your bosom.
SHYLOCK   Ay, his breast.
    So says the bond, doth it not, noble judge?
    'Nearest his heart': those are the very words.   250
PORTIA It is so. Are there balance here to weigh
    The flesh?
SHYLOCK   I have them ready.
PORTIA Have by some surgeon, Shylock, on your charge,
    To stop his wounds, lest he do bleed to death.
SHYLOCK Is it so nominated in the bond?   255
PORTIA It is not so expressed, but what of that?
    'Twere good you do so much for charity.
SHYLOCK I cannot find it, 'tis not in the bond.
PORTIA You, merchant: have you anything to say?
ANTONIO But little; I am armed and well prepared.   260
    Give me your hand, Bassanio. Fare you well.
    Grieve not that I am fall'n to this for you.
    For herein Fortune shows herself more kind
    Than is her custom: it is still her use
    To let the wretched man outlive his wealth,   265
    To view with hollow eye and wrinkled brow
    An age of poverty; from which ling'ring penance
    Of such misery doth she cut me off.
    Commend me to your honourable wife.
    Tell her the process of Antonio's end,   270
    Say how I loved you, speak me fair in death,
    And when the tale is told, bid her be judge
    Whether Bassanio had not once a love.
    Repent but you that you shall lose your friend
    And he repents not that he pays your debt.   275
    For if the Jew do cut but deep enough
    I'll pay it instantly with all my heart.

Portia gives judgement in Shylock's favour but, at the last moment, saves Antonio. Blood is not mentioned in the bond, so Shylock must break the law if he sheds Antonio's.

---

1 They wish their wives were dead! (in groups of four)

Both Bassanio (lines 278–83) and Gratiano (lines 286–8) would sacrifice their wives for Antonio. The audience knows (but the two men don't) that Portia and Nerissa are listening. In the middle of what looks like a tragic scene, Shakespeare lightens the mood. Talk together about how he uses Portia's and Nerissa's disguises to humorous effect, and why he changes the emotional balance of the scene at this point.

2 'Come, prepare' (in groups of three)

Line 300 contains the climactic moment of the trial scene. It is almost unbearably tense as Antonio waits, his bare chest exposed, for Shylock to wield his knife (see picture on p. xi). Only after agonising suspense does Portia break the silence to deny Shylock's murderous intent. How near is Shylock to cutting Antonio when Portia stops him? Take parts as Shylock, Portia and Antonio and experiment with different ways of presenting the drama that unfolds between lines 300 and 301. Share your versions with other groups.

3 Portia's coup . . . 'Tarry a little' (in pairs)

Portia must have known all along about this loophole in Shylock's bond. First, share a reading of lines 294–300, bringing out the game of cat and mouse which Portia is obviously playing with Shylock. Then concentrate on lines 301–8. Work on how the words should be spoken, and how Shylock should react.

---

esteemed valued
currish dog-like
else otherwise
stock family
Barabbas a Jewish thief pardoned by Pontius Pilate instead of Jesus

trifle waste
Tarry wait
urgest demand

BASSANIO Antonio, I am married to a wife
　　　　Which is as dear to me as life itself;
　　　　But life itself, my wife, and all the world,　　　　　　280
　　　　Are not with me esteemed above thy life.
　　　　I would lose all, ay, sacrifice them all
　　　　Here to this devil, to deliver you.
PORTIA Your wife would give you little thanks for that
　　　　If she were by to hear you make the offer.　　　　　　285
GRATIANO I have a wife who I protest I love;
　　　　I would she were in heaven, so she could
　　　　Entreat some power to change this currish Jew.
NERISSA 'Tis well you offer it behind her back;
　　　　The wish would make else an unquiet house.　　　　　290
SHYLOCK These be the Christian husbands! I have a daughter:
　　　　Would any of the stock of Barabbas
　　　　Had been her husband, rather than a Christian!
　　　　We trifle time; I pray thee pursue sentence.
PORTIA A pound of that same merchant's flesh is thine,　　　295
　　　　The court awards it, and the law doth give it.
SHYLOCK Most rightful judge!
PORTIA And you must cut this flesh from off his breast;
　　　　The law allows it, and the court awards it.
SHYLOCK Most learned judge! A sentence: come, prepare.　　　300
PORTIA Tarry a little, there is something else.
　　　　This bond doth give thee here no jot of blood.
　　　　The words expressly are 'a pound of flesh'.
　　　　Take then thy bond, take thou thy pound of flesh,
　　　　But in the cutting it, if thou dost shed　　　　　　305
　　　　One drop of Christian blood, thy lands and goods
　　　　Are by the laws of Venice confiscate
　　　　Unto the state of Venice.
GRATIANO　　　　　　　　　　O upright judge!
　　　　Mark, Jew – O learned judge!
SHYLOCK Is that the law?
PORTIA　　　　　　　　　Thyself shall see the Act.　　　　310
　　　　For as thou urgest justice, be assured
　　　　Thou shalt have justice more than thou desirest.

Shylock is defeated, and Portia insists on justice. She will not allow him to be repaid any money, only to take the pound of flesh at his peril.

---

1 Portia in control (in groups of four to six)

Shylock, sensing that victory is slipping away, agrees to accept a financial settlement of his bond. Bassanio is prepared to hand over the money, but Portia insists that 'justice' must prevail and that Shylock must exact the penalty. She shows that she is more than equal to the men of Venice.

a Read over Portia's speeches on the opposite page. Work out gestures you could use to accompany each statement she makes.

b Choose three quotations to show that Portia is in charge of events.

c Talk about whether you admire Portia's assertiveness. Women have little freedom in Venice, but is she setting a good example to other women in her treatment of Shylock?

2 Peripeteia: a reversal of fortune (in pairs)

A few moments ago, Shylock seemed triumphant, but now Portia has turned the tables on him. It is an example of **peripeteia** (a reversal of fortune), a term which originates in ancient Greek tragedy. Portia is determined to punish him for his treatment of Antonio. Read aloud only Shylock's words from line 294 to line 342, and trace the stages of his decline and loss of dignity. Present this in visual or diagrammatic form.

3 Gratiano rubs salt in

Gratiano is pleased to use Shylock's own words against him (lines 319, 329 and 336). Find Shylock's original expressions in this scene. Line 330 also echoes an earlier expression of Shylock's (in Act 1 Scene 3). Practise speaking the four lines aloud to convey Gratiano's pleasure at Shylock's discomfort. Decide on gestures to go with Gratiano's taunts (does 'on the hip' refer to where Shylock keeps his purse?). Do these lines confirm your earlier impression of Gratiano?

---

thrice three times over
Soft not so fast
penalty the pound of flesh
As makes . . . scruple even if it's just by a fraction
scruple gram

principal the original sum owed (3,000 ducats)
the devil . . . it he's welcome to it
I'll stay . . . question I'm not staying to argue about this

GRATIANO O learned judge! Mark, Jew: a learned judge.
SHYLOCK I take this offer then. Pay the bond thrice
      And let the Christian go.
BASSANIO   Here is the money.   315
PORTIA Soft.
      The Jew shall have all justice; soft, no haste;
      He shall have nothing but the penalty.
GRATIANO O Jew, an upright judge, a learned judge!
PORTIA Therefore prepare thee to cut off the flesh.   320
      Shed thou no blood, nor cut thou less nor more
      But just a pound of flesh. If thou tak'st more
      Or less than a just pound, be it but so much
      As makes it light or heavy in the substance
      Or the division of the twentieth part   325
      Of one poor scruple – nay, if the scale do turn
      But in the estimation of a hair,
      Thou diest, and all thy goods are confiscate.
GRATIANO A second Daniel; a Daniel, Jew!
      Now, infidel, I have you on the hip.   330
PORTIA Why doth the Jew pause? Take thy forfeiture.
SHYLOCK Give me my principal, and let me go.
BASSANIO I have it ready for thee; here it is.
PORTIA He hath refused it in the open court.
      He shall have merely justice and his bond.   335
GRATIANO A Daniel, still say I, a second Daniel!
      I thank thee, Jew, for teaching me that word.
SHYLOCK Shall I not have barely my principal?
PORTIA Thou shalt have nothing but the forfeiture,
      To be so taken at thy peril, Jew.   340
SHYLOCK Why then, the devil give him good of it!
      I'll stay no longer question.

Portia reveals another trap for Shylock. If a foreigner plots to kill a Venetian, the punishment by law should be confiscation of all their wealth, and their possible execution.

---

1 The laws of Venice (individually and in pairs)

a **Portia's legal language**   Portia's words (lines 342–59) sound almost as if she is reading from the laws of Venice. Rewrite her speech in your own words, as if you have to explain to a friend the details of how Shylock has broken the law and how he might be punished.

b **Is the law fair?**   Improvise an argument about the law Shylock has broken. One person should be a native Venetian, the other a member of a non-Christian group living in Venice. How does an 'alien' feel about such possible treatment at the hands of the law? How can a Venetian justify such legal prejudice?

2 Gratiano's at it again (in pairs)

Shylock is ordered by Portia to kneel to the Duke and plead for mercy. But Gratiano again abuses Shylock. Take turns to be Gratiano and Shylock. Experiment with how lines 360–3 might be spoken. Try the words in as many different ways as possible, and talk about the dramatic effects you wish to achieve.

3 Is this the final blow? (in groups of four or five)

Shylock is devastated by the loss of his wealth. Devise a mime or tableau to represent the anguish expressed in lines 371–3. You may wish to have a narrator speaking the lines as you present your mime or tableau.

---

enacted   stated
alien   foreigner
The party . . . contrive   the person who is plotted against
privy coffer   the Duke's personal fortune
'gainst all other voice   without appeal
by manifest proceeding   obvious

danger . . . rehearsed   the punishments I've just explained
leave   permission
spirit   natures
You take . . . house   you destroy my family when you remove my means of supporting my home
halter gratis   hangman's noose for free

PORTIA   Tarry, Jew:
    The law hath yet another hold on you.
    It is enacted in the laws of Venice,
    If it be proved against an alien   345
    That by direct or indirect attempts
    He seek the life of any citizen,
    The party 'gainst the which he doth contrive
    Shall seize one half his goods, the other half
    Comes to the privy coffer of the state,   350
    And the offender's life lies in the mercy
    Of the Duke only, 'gainst all other voice.
    In which predicament I say thou stand'st;
    For it appears by manifest proceeding
    That indirectly, and directly too,   355
    Thou hast contrived against the very life
    Of the defendant, and thou hast incurred
    The danger formerly by me rehearsed.
    Down, therefore, and beg mercy of the Duke.
GRATIANO Beg that thou mayst have leave to hang thyself –   360
    And yet, thy wealth being forfeit to the state,
    Thou hast not left the value of a cord;
    Therefore thou must be hanged at the state's charge.
DUKE That thou shalt see the difference of our spirit,
    I pardon thee thy life before thou ask it.   365
    For half thy wealth, it is Antonio's;
    The other half comes to the general state,
    Which humbleness may drive unto a fine.
PORTIA Ay, for the state, not for Antonio.
SHYLOCK Nay, take my life and all, pardon not that: 370
    You take my house when you do take the prop
    That doth sustain my house; you take my life
    When you do take the means whereby I live.
PORTIA What mercy can you render him, Antonio?
GRATIANO A halter gratis – nothing else, for God's sake.   375

Antonio requests – and is granted – partial mercy for Shylock: he can keep half his wealth; Antonio will invest the rest. Unwittingly, Bassanio tries to reward Portia with her own money.

---

1 Shylock's punishment: a summary (in pairs)

Use lines 376–86 to make a diagram, illustrating in words and pictures Antonio's suggestions for the punishment of Shylock. Find a clear way of showing the order in which they might rank as humiliations in Shylock's mind.

2 Antonio: a merciful Christian? (in small groups)

Talk together about Antonio's treatment of Shylock. Has he given up the vicious prejudice of his past, or are these reduced punishments (lines 376–86) still calculated to inflict misery and humiliation on Shylock? In particular, discuss the demand that Shylock becomes a Christian, an instruction that would be deeply offensive to Shylock (because his religion specifically prohibits such conversion).

3 Shylock: the final curtain (in pairs)

A director said that Shylock should speak his last lines 'with all the ruefulness of a man who realises he's made a very silly mistake . . . to take on the establishment and play it at its own game . . .'. The actor playing Shylock must decide how to leave the stage speaking his final, virtually monosyllabic lines (390, 391–3). Sometimes he exits with great dignity, sometimes as a broken man. Laurence Olivier as Shylock made his exit in a dignified manner, but after he'd gone off, a long, agonised scream was heard.

First, explore reading the lines in a variety of ways. Then, as director, write instructions for Shylock about how he should leave the stage.

---

have . . . use   invest the other half
record a gift   sign a deed of gift
of all . . . possessed   everything he
  owns when he dies
Had . . . more   if I'd had my way, you'd
  have been in front of a jury

meet   necessary
leisure   time
gratify   reward
bound   in debt
in lieu whereof   in place of which
cope   give in exchange for

ANTONIO So please my lord the Duke and all the court
    To quit the fine for one half of his goods,
    I am content, so he will let me have
    The other half in use, to render it
    Upon his death unto the gentleman   380
    That lately stole his daughter.
    Two things provided more: that for this favour
    He presently become a Christian;
    The other, that he do record a gift,
    Here in the court, of all he dies possessed   385
    Unto his son Lorenzo and his daughter.
DUKE He shall do this, or else I do recant
    The pardon that I late pronouncèd here.
PORTIA Art thou contented, Jew? What dost thou say?
SHYLOCK I am content.
PORTIA   Clerk, draw a deed of gift.   390
SHYLOCK I pray you give me leave to go from hence;
    I am not well. Send the deed after me
    And I will sign it.
DUKE   Get thee gone, but do it.
GRATIANO In christening shalt thou have two godfathers:
    Had I been judge, thou shouldst have had ten more,   395
    To bring thee to the gallows, not to the font.
                           Exit [Shylock]
DUKE Sir, I entreat you home with me to dinner.
PORTIA I humbly do desire your grace of pardon.
    I must away this night toward Padua,
    And it is meet I presently set forth.   400
DUKE I am sorry that your leisure serves you not.
    Antonio, gratify this gentleman,
    For in my mind you are much bound to him.
                        Exit Duke and his train
BASSANIO Most worthy gentleman, I and my friend
    Have by your wisdom been this day acquitted   405
    Of grievous penalties, in lieu whereof
    Three thousand ducats due unto the Jew
    We freely cope your courteous pains withal.
ANTONIO And stand indebted over and above
    In love and service to you evermore.   410

Portia refuses money, but asks insistently for Bassanio's ring: the very one she gave him in Act 3, saying then that its loss would mark the end of his love for her. Bassanio cannot part with it, and Portia mocks him.

1 Nerissa: in on Portia's secret (in groups of three)

Once again Shakespeare uses dramatic irony to add a further twist to the plot (this time for comic effect). Unlike Bassanio and Antonio, Nerissa and the audience know Portia's true identity. Two people read aloud the whole of the opposite page; the third stops them at lines or phrases which might bring a smile to Nerissa's lips. Several of Portia's remarks have much greater significance for Nerissa than for the two men and because she does not take part in the dialogue she can more easily convey her amusement to the audience.

After your reading, talk together about the comic possibilities that Portia's comments give to the actors on stage. Also explore how this humorous interlude might alter the audience's response after what has gone before.

2 Portia's dominance grows (in pairs)

Portia insists on having the ring (line 428). She knows its importance and the anguish its loss will cause Bassanio. Why does she deal with her husband with the same ruthlessness as she has shown to Shylock? Talk together about whether she is cruel or wise in setting this test for Bassanio. Think of other explanations for her insisting on having the ring. Jot down possible reasons, and compare them with other groups.

As Portia and Nerissa leave at line 444, improvise or script a conversation that they have about the dramatic events in the court-room. What will Portia make of her victories? And of the test of her husband's love that she has just set up?

---

delivering saving
My . . . mercenary I don't care about money
know recognise or have sex with (a pun for Nerissa's benefit?)
of force . . . further I must persuade you more

remembrance memento
trifle trinket
proclamation public announcement
liberal generous
scuse excuse

PORTIA He is well paid that is well satisfied;
        And I delivering you am satisfied
        And therein do account myself well paid;
        My mind was never yet more mercenary.
        I pray you know me when we meet again.   415
        I wish you well, and so I take my leave.
BASSANIO Dear sir, of force I must attempt you further.
        Take some remembrance of us as a tribute,
        Not as a fee. Grant me two things, I pray you:
        Not to deny me, and to pardon me.   420
PORTIA You press me far, and therefore I will yield.
        Give me your gloves, I'll wear them for your sake;
        And for your love I'll take this ring from you.
        Do not draw back your hand; I'll take no more,
        And you in love shall not deny me this.   425
BASSANIO This ring, good sir? Alas, it is a trifle;
        I will not shame myself to give you this.
PORTIA I will have nothing else but only this;
        And now methinks I have a mind to it.
BASSANIO There's more depends on this than on the value.   430
        The dearest ring in Venice will I give you,
        And find it out by proclamation.
        Only for this I pray you pardon me.
PORTIA I see, sir, you are liberal in offers.
        You taught me first to beg, and now methinks   435
        You teach me how a beggar should be answered.
BASSANIO Good sir, this ring was given me by my wife,
        And when she put it on, she made me vow
        That I should neither sell, nor give, nor lose it.
PORTIA That scuse serves many men to save their gifts;   440
        And if your wife be not a mad woman,
        And know how well I have deserved this ring,
        She would not hold out enemy for ever
        For giving it to me. Well, peace be with you.
                        Exeunt [Portia and Nerissa]

Antonio persuades Bassanio to part with the ring. Gratiano brings it to Portia. Nerissa plans to set the same test for her husband by making him give her his ring too.

---

1 Friendship versus marriage vow

Antonio persuades Bassanio to reward Balthazar (Portia) by handing over his ring. Bassanio gives in without comment (line 448), under-lining that his friend's wish has more power than the vow he gave to his wife. What does this suggest about Bassanio's strength of feeling for Antonio?

2 Nerissa's perspectives (in pairs and individually)

a **Extending the joke**   Nerissa and Gratiano are on their way to Shylock's house. Improvise their conversation in which Nerissa (in disguise) has to persuade her husband to give away his ring to someone he thinks is Balthazar's clerk. . . .

b **At Shylock's house**   Nerissa is sent to Shylock's house (lines 1 and 11) for him to sign the deed of gift, naming Jessica and Lorenzo as his heirs. As Nerissa, write your own account of the visit. How does Shylock receive you? How has the trial affected him? How do you respond?

3 A third trial ahead

After the 'trial' of the caskets and the 'trial' of Shylock, Shakespeare now sets a third 'trial' plot in motion (the rings). Read Portia's lines 15–17. Portia anticipates that she and Nerissa will be able to force grovelling confessions from their husbands when they meet up again. Think about the deceptions that the two women have just practised and write a paragraph on your response to what they have done and intend to do.

Let his . . . commandement   weigh what he deserves plus my love against what your wife orders
presently   immediately
Fair . . . o'ertane   I'm glad I've caught up with you

entreat   beg
I warrant   I'm sure
old (line 15)   incredible
outface them   be cheekier than them, stare them down
tarry   wait for you

ANTONIO My lord Bassanio, let him have the ring.   445
       Let his deservings and my love withal
       Be valued 'gainst your wife's commandement.
BASSANIO Go, Gratiano, run and overtake him;
       Give him the ring, and bring him if thou canst
       Unto Antonio's house. Away, make haste.   450

                                               Exit Gratiano

       Come, you and I will thither presently,
       And in the morning early will we both
       Fly toward Belmont. Come, Antonio.   *Exeunt*

Act 4 Scene 2
Venice A street

Enter PORTIA and NERISSA

PORTIA Enquire the Jew's house out, give him this deed,
       And let him sign it. We'll away tonight
       And be a day before our husbands home.
       This deed will be well welcome to Lorenzo.

Enter GRATIANO

GRATIANO Fair sir, you are well o'ertane.   5
       My lord Bassanio upon more advice
       Hath sent you here this ring, and doth entreat
       Your company at dinner.
PORTIA   That cannot be.
       His ring I do accept most thankfully,
       And so I pray you tell him. Furthermore,   10
       I pray you show my youth old Shylock's house.
GRATIANO That will I do.
NERISSA   *[To Portia]* Sir, I would speak with you.
       [Aside] I'll see if I can get my husband's ring
       Which I did make him swear to keep for ever.
PORTIA Thou mayst, I warrant. We shall have old swearing   15
       That they did give the rings away to men;
       But we'll outface them, and outswear them too.
       – Away, make haste, thou know'st where I will tarry.
NERISSA Come, good sir, will you show me to this house?   *[Exeunt]*

Looking back at Act 4
Activities for groups or individuals

1 A fair trial?

The long trial scene which occupies virtually all of Act 4 has often been judged to be the heart of the play. It is the best-known episode and the climactic turning point of the drama. The tables are turned on Shylock, his thirst for revenge is confounded and he is utterly humiliated.

a The trial scene displays the struggle between justice and mercy. Write a paragraph exploring the balance between justice and mercy in:

  • the major characters' contributions to the scene
  • the final outcome of the trial.

b Does Shylock receive a fair trial? Consider this from the point of view of:

  • the State of Venice
  • Shylock
  • yourself.

Give reasons to justify your findings.

c Run through a list of characters who appear in Act 4. Put them in order of:

  • how much you respect them
  • how much prejudice you think they show
  • how much you like them.

How far do the lists match?

2 Antonio's last letter

Imagine you are Antonio. It is just before the trial. Write your last letter to Bassanio, to be read after your death.

3 The knife and the scales

These props are of great significance in Scene 1. Design your ideal versions of Shylock's knife and set of scales. Try to achieve theatrical impact with your design, and ensure that both items are convincing possessions of Shylock.

4 'Give me some lines!'

In defeat, Shylock, normally a man of many words, says little. Dustin Hoffman, an actor who played Shylock, said, 'Halfway through the trial Portia takes over and Shakespeare doesn't give me anything to say . . . if he was still alive, I'd be saying "Give me some lines!"'

You are given the chance to write one extra speech for Shylock. At what point would you include it, and what would he say?

5 Which line?

Portia confronts the seated Shylock. Identify the point in the script at which you think this dramatic moment occurred. In what historical period have the director and designer set this production?

Lorenzo and Jessica are reminded by the moonlit night of famous lovers from classical mythology. They speak, somewhat ambiguously, of their love for each other.

---

1 'The moon shines bright' (in pairs)

a Take parts and read the opposite page aloud. Concentrate on the patterning of the verse ('In such a night' is repeated eight times) and how the shared lines and balanced phrases suggest a mood of harmony and romance.

b Talk together about the contrasts between the opening to this scene and the drama of the trial scene in the previous act.

2 Classical lovers (in groups of three or four)

a The moon is shining brightly, the sweet wind kisses the trees. In this perfect setting, Jessica and Lorenzo recall the deeds of famous (but unfortunate) lovers on 'such a night':

- Troilus climbed the walls of Troy to be with his lover Cressida. She later betrayed him.
- Thisbe met her lover Pyramus secretly and against her father's wishes. Their love pact ended in suicide.
- Dido, queen of Carthage, spent a night like this on the shore trying to entice her lover, Aeneas, back to her. But he had deserted her.
- Medea gathered enchanted herbs to refresh Aeson, the father of her lover Jason, whom she had helped to win the Golden Fleece. She was later deserted by him.

Compile a chart showing how these tales of tragedy, betrayal and loss are reflected by events in *The Merchant of Venice*.

b In lines 14–23, Lorenzo and Jessica speak rather ambiguously of their relationship. Lorenzo (lines 14–17) adds Jessica to the list of unfortunate lovers. Read the lines then talk together about what they add to your understanding of their relationship.

Troilus   son of King Priam of Troy, betrayed by his lover Cressida

Thisbe   frightened by a lion, she never met her lover Pyramus

Dido   queen of Carthage, deserted by Aeneas

waft   beckoned to

Medea   she ran away with her lover, Jason, but was deserted

Aeson   Jason's father

unthrift   generous

shrew   small mouse-like animal, or a bad-tempered woman

outnight   go on, outlast

Act 5 Scene 1
Belmont   Portia's garden

Enter LORENZO *and* JESSICA

LORENZO The moon shines bright. In such a night as this,
       When the sweet wind did gently kiss the trees,
       And they did make no noise, in such a night
       Troilus methinks mounted the Troyan walls
       And sighed his soul toward the Grecian tents,   5
       Where Cressid lay that night.

JESSICA   In such a night
       Did Thisbe fearfully o'ertrip the dew,
       And saw the lion's shadow ere himself,
       And ran dismayed away.

LORENZO   In such a night
       Stood Dido with a willow in her hand   10
       Upon the wild sea banks, and waft her love
       To come again to Carthage.

JESSICA   In such a night
       Medea gathered the enchanted herbs
       That did renew old Aeson.

LORENZO   In such a night
       Did Jessica steal from the wealthy Jew   15
       And with an unthrift love did run from Venice
       As far as Belmont.

JESSICA   In such a night
       Did young Lorenzo swear he loved her well,
       Stealing her soul with many vows of faith,
       And ne'er a true one.

LORENZO   In such a night   20
       Did pretty Jessica (like a little shrew)
       Slander her love, and he forgave it her.

JESSICA I would outnight you, did nobody come:
       But hark, I hear the footing of a man.

Stephano brings news of Portia's imminent return to Belmont. Lancelot informs Lorenzo that Bassanio is also on his way home. Lorenzo proposes to welcome them with music.

---

1 Has Portia found God? (in pairs)

Portia seems to have been very religious on her way back from Venice. She has stopped to pray at holy places and is accompanied by a holy hermit.

a Talk about possible explanations for Portia's religious behaviour after her triumph in Venice. Since the 'holy hermit' never appears, do you think it might be another of her fictitious inventions?

b Portia is praying for a happy marriage (line 32). What do you think she would be hoping for from marriage to Bassanio? Talk about your ideas, then write a dramatic soliloquy which captures some of her hopes and dreams. You could write it in the form of a prayer.

2 A welcome-home party (in small groups)

Lorenzo plans to welcome Portia home with a celebration. Remember the mood established at the opening of this scene, and the importance of Portia's return. What will the welcome be like? Talk about this, then prepare a short routine (one or two minutes long) which celebrates Portia's homecoming. You could produce a short improvised play, a mime, a song, instrumental music, a dance or a poem, for example. Each group's welcoming activity can become part of a whole-class presentation.

3 Lancelot and Lorenzo – comic confusion (in pairs)

Read lines 39–45. Here are two characters who cannot seem to find each other in the darkness! Try to memorise the lines and play the short sequence wearing blindfolds or with your eyes closed. Add movements and work on bringing out the humour and confusion.

Sola / Wo ha	hunting cries	**expect**	await
post	messenger	**signify**	inform people

Enter [STEPHANO,] *a messenger*

LORENZO Who comes so fast in silence of the night?   25
STEPHANO A friend.
LORENZO A friend? What friend? Your name, I pray you, friend?
STEPHANO Stephano is my name, and I bring word
         My mistress will before the break of day
         Be here at Belmont. She doth stray about   30
         By holy crosses where she kneels and prays
         For happy wedlock hours.
LORENZO   Who comes with her?
STEPHANO None but a holy hermit and her maid.
         I pray you, is my master yet returned?
LORENZO He is not, nor we have not heard from him.   35
         But go we in, I pray thee, Jessica,
         And ceremoniously let us prepare
         Some welcome for the mistress of the house.

Enter [LANCELOT,] *the Clown*

LANCELOT Sola, sola! Wo ha, ho! Sola, sola!
LORENZO Who calls?   40
LANCELOT Sola! Did you see Master Lorenzo? Master Lorenzo, sola,
    sola!
LORENZO Leave holloaing, man! Here!
LANCELOT Sola! Where, where?
LORENZO Here!   45
LANCELOT Tell him there's a post come from my master, with his horn
    full of good news: my master will be here ere morning, sweet
    soul.
LORENZO Let's in and there expect their coming.
         And yet no matter: why should we go in?   50
         My friend Stephano, signify I pray you,
         Within the house, your mistress is at hand,
         And bring your music forth into the air.
                                [*Exit Stephano*]

Lorenzo tells Jessica of the harmony of the heavens. As the musicians play, he describes the healing powers of music.

---

1 The music of the spheres (in small groups)

Lorenzo's lines 54–68 describe 'the music of the spheres': the ancient belief that moving stars and planets revolved on crystal spheres and made heavenly music as they orbited. Work on some of the following:

a Read aloud lines 54–68, each person reading a short, meaningful unit of the script. Emphasise all the words connected with the senses; on a second reading, those connected with religion. Try other ways of reading in order to bring out the melodious, dreamlike and romantic mood of the verse.

b Lorenzo is saddened that humans, who are imperfect, cannot hear the heavenly music (lines 64–5). Jessica, in line 69, admits that music does not cheer her, even though Lorenzo assures her of its healing powers. Talk together about what might cause them to feel so differently.

c Read Lorenzo's lines 70–88 several times. He describes the powerful effects music can have on any listener. Wild animals are entranced by soothing music. Orpheus, a legendary Greek, used music to charm trees, stones and floods. Music has healing powers and any man who does not respond to it must be villainous and untrustworthy (line 85). Discuss whether you agree with Lorenzo that people who cannot respond to music are 'fit for treasons, stratagems, and spoils'.

d Improvise a short scene to show Lorenzo's belief that music can dramatically transform frantic or brutal moods and behaviour.

e Look back to Shylock's lines (Act 2 Scene 5, lines 27–35) in which he described the music of Christian masques as 'shallow foppery'. Talk together about how Lorenzo's lines 70–88 implicitly criticise Shylock's values and attitude.

Become fit
patens small plates (used at Holy Communion)
orb star
choiring singing
cherubins beautiful angels
muddy vesture of decay human body
Diana the moon goddess

Fetching mad bounds jumping
mutual stand stop all together
Orpheus a legendary Greek whose music enchanted
stockish insensitive
spoils plunder
Erebus a dark place near hell

How sweet the moonlight sleeps upon this bank!
Here will we sit, and let the sounds of music   55
Creep in our ears; soft stillness and the night
Become the touches of sweet harmony.
Sit, Jessica. Look how the floor of heaven
Is thick inlaid with patens of bright gold.
There's not the smallest orb which thou behold'st   60
But in his motion like an angel sings,
Still choiring to the young-eyed cherubins.
Such harmony is in immortal souls,
But whilst this muddy vesture of decay
Doth grossly close it in, we cannot hear it.   65

[*Enter* STEPHANO *with musicians*]

Come, ho! and wake Diana with a hymn.
With sweetest touches pierce your mistress' ear,
And draw her home with music.
                        Music plays
JESSICA I am never merry when I hear sweet music.
LORENZO The reason is your spirits are attentive.   70
For do but note a wild and wanton herd
Or race of youthful and unhandled colts
Fetching mad bounds, bellowing and neighing loud –
Which is the hot condition of their blood –
If they but hear perchance a trumpet sound,   75
Or any air of music touch their ears,
You shall perceive them make a mutual stand,
Their savage eyes turned to a modest gaze
By the sweet power of music. Therefore the poet
Did feign that Orpheus drew trees, stones, and floods;   80
Since naught so stockish, hard, and full of rage,
But music for the time doth change his nature.
The man that hath no music in himself,
Nor is not moved with concord of sweet sounds,
Is fit for treasons, stratagems, and spoils;   85
The motions of his spirit are dull as night
And his affections dark as Erebus.
Let no such man be trusted. Mark the music.

Portia and Nerissa return, unnoticed at first, and comment on the light and the music. They discover that their husbands have not yet arrived in Belmont, and plan to keep quiet about their own absence.

---

1 'So shines a good deed in a naughty world' (in groups)

Portia's lines 89–91 echo words spoken by Jesus in St Matthew's Gospel (Matthew 5: 14–16), which include the phrase 'Let your light so shine before men'. She seems to be associating herself with 'light' (shining from her hall) in a symbolic way. Is the 'good deed' she speaks of (line 91) the saving of Antonio?

- Talk together about the possible importance of this speech in shaping your impression of Portia.
- After your discussion, make a tableau to illustrate Portia's line 91.

2 Relative values (in pairs)

Portia in her speeches from line 93 to line 110 insists that only comparisons can reveal the true worth of anything. The comparisons that she makes include measuring the relative values of a substitute against a real king, and an inland river against the sea. Take turns to read her lines, then say whether (and why / why not) you agree that 'Nothing is good . . . without respect [comparison]'. It will help if you give actual examples.

3 A secret entrance? (in groups of three)

Take parts and read the page opposite. Stop at the point where you think Portia and Nerissa are recognised. Work out how you would arrange the characters on stage for this part of the scene. Remember that Lorenzo, Jessica, Stephano and the musicians are already on stage, even though they don't speak whilst Portia and Nerissa are conversing. Decide upon the most dramatically effective moment and manner of their entrance and 'discovery'.

---

naughty worthless, wicked
main of waters the ocean
respect comparison
attended in company
season appropriate time

Endymion a beautiful youth, loved by the moon goddess, Diana (perhaps Portia points to Lorenzo and Jessica, asleep)

Enter PORTIA *and* NERISSA

PORTIA That light we see is burning in my hall.
How far that little candle throws his beams!   90
So shines a good deed in a naughty world.
NERISSA When the moon shone we did not see the candle.
PORTIA So doth the greater glory dim the less:
A substitute shines brightly as a king
Until a king be by, and then his state   95
Empties itself, as doth an inland brook
Into the main of waters. Music, hark!
NERISSA It is your music, madam, of the house.
PORTIA Nothing is good, I see, without respect;
Methinks it sounds much sweeter than by day.   100
NERISSA Silence bestows that virtue on it, madam.
PORTIA The crow doth sing as sweetly as the lark
When neither is attended; and I think
The nightingale, if she should sing by day
When every goose is cackling, would be thought   105
No better a musician than the wren.
How many things by season seasoned are
To their right praise and true perfection.
Peace, ho! The moon sleeps with Endymion
And would not be awaked!
                    [*Music ceases*]
LORENZO   That is the voice,   110
Or I am much deceived, of Portia!
PORTIA He knows me as the blind man knows the cuckoo
By the bad voice.
LORENZO   Dear lady, welcome home!
PORTIA We have been praying for our husbands' welfare,
Which speed we hope the better for our words.   115
Are they returned?
LORENZO   Madam, they are not yet.
But there is come a messenger before
To signify their coming.
PORTIA   Go in, Nerissa:
Give order to my servants that they take
No note at all of our being absent hence –   120
Nor you Lorenzo, Jessica nor you.

Bassanio returns with Antonio and Gratiano. Nerissa challenges Gratiano. He has given away her ring, which he swore to wear as long as he lived!

---

1 Antonio in Belmont

This is Antonio's only visit to Belmont. The traumatic experience of his trial is only recently behind him. What do you think will be in his mind as he arrives? He gives only a brief insight into his thoughts at line 138. Use your own ideas to write a monologue for Antonio.

2 Husbands versus wives (in groups of five)

a **An argument begins**   There will be much embarrassment for Gratiano and Bassanio as they try to explain why they've given away their wives' rings. To enjoy the domestic quarrels, take parts as the husbands and wives and Antonio (who can double as Lorenzo), and read quickly through to the end of the play.

b **Portia's teasing wordplay**   Portia can't help teasing Bassanio. When she uses the word 'light' in line 130, she puns on its meaning as 'unfaithful'. Another pun on 'bound' in line 136 echoes Antonio's imprisonment and Bassanio's financial debt to him. Talk together about Portia's wordplay. Is it comic, serious or barbed?

c **'You do me wrong!'**   A quarrel breaks out at line 142 between Nerissa and Gratiano. She accuses him that despite all his vows he has given his ring to 'a judge's clerk'. But how did Nerissa 'notice' that Gratiano had lost the ring? Work in pairs and improvise the way their conversation began, developing it as far as 'By yonder moon . . .' (line 142).

d **'A paltry ring'**   Nerissa (lines 151–6) declares that the intrinsic worth of the ring is not important. What matters is the love pledge that it represents. Suggest how this adds to your understanding of the value systems of Venice and Belmont.

---

the Antipodes   the other side of the world
light   wanton, unfaithful
scant   cut short
gelt   castrated

poesy   motto
cutler's poetry   poor-quality verse
You should . . . respective   You should have respected the circumstances under which it was given

[*A tucket sounds*]

LORENZO Your husband is at hand, I hear his trumpet.
        We are no telltales, madam; fear you not.

PORTIA This night methinks is but the daylight sick,
        It looks a little paler; 'tis a day   125
        Such as the day is when the sun is hid.

Enter BASSANIO, ANTONIO, GRATIANO, *and their followers*

BASSANIO We should hold day with the Antipodes,
        If you would walk in absence of the sun.

PORTIA Let me give light, but let me not be light,
        For a light wife doth make a heavy husband,   130
        And never be Bassanio so for me –
        But God sort all! You are welcome home, my lord.

BASSANIO I thank you, madam. Give welcome to my friend.
        This is the man, this is Antonio,
        To whom I am so infinitely bound.   135

PORTIA You should in all sense be much bound to him,
        For as I hear he was much bound for you.

ANTONIO No more than I am well acquitted of.

PORTIA Sir, you are very welcome to our house.
        It must appear in other ways than words: 140
        Therefore I scant this breathing courtesy.

GRATIANO [*To Nerissa*] By yonder moon I swear you do me wrong!
        In faith, I gave it to the judge's clerk,
        Would he were gelt that had it, for my part,
        Since you do take it, love, so much at heart.   145

PORTIA A quarrel ho, already! What's the matter?

GRATIANO About a hoop of gold, a paltry ring
        That she did give me, whose poesy was
        For all the world like cutler's poetry
        Upon a knife: 'Love me, and leave me not.'   150

NERISSA What talk you of the poesy or the value?
        You swore to me when I did give it you.
        That you would wear it till your hour of death,
        And that it should lie with you in your grave.
        Though not for me, yet for your vehement oaths   155
        You should have been respective and have kept it.
        Gave it a judge's clerk! No, God's my judge
        The clerk will ne'er wear hair on's face that had it.

Gratiano insists that he gave the ring to the judge's clerk. Portia reproaches him, saying that Bassanio would never have parted with her ring. Gratiano tells Portia that's exactly what Bassanio has done.

---

1 Portia: another 'cat and mouse' performance (in groups of three)

Portia and Nerissa are in a conspiracy with the audience. It's another occasion when the audience knows more than most of the other characters – in this case, Bassanio and Gratiano. Portia's lines 166–76 sound very serious to the two husbands, but are very amusing to the audience. She already has the ring in her possession, and she wants to make Bassanio squirm! Bassanio must be feeling very guilty: Gratiano is being reprimanded for the same misdeed that he has committed. His agitation comes to the surface in his Aside (lines 177–8) and continues as Gratiano reveals that he's given away Portia's ring.

a Take parts as Portia, Bassanio and Gratiano. Read lines 161–91. As one person speaks, the other two react appropriately, especially showing the expressions that appear on the men's faces. Practise different readings and reactions. Decide which are most effective. Use pauses and timing to increase the comic impact of the sequence.

b If this were a cartoon strip, what would be written in Bassanio's thought bubbles while he is listening to Gratiano giving him away to Portia?

2 Bassanio's honesty (in pairs)

When Bassanio is forced to admit that he no longer has the ring, he does so without excuses. Talk together about whether you feel you see a different side to his character here.

---

scrubbèd stunted
prating talkative

aught anything

GRATIANO He will, and if he live to be a man.

NERISSA Ay, if a woman live to be a man.   160

GRATIANO Now by this hand, I gave it to a youth,
    A kind of boy, a little scrubbèd boy
    No higher than thyself, the judge's clerk,
    A prating boy that begged it as a fee;
    I could not for my heart deny it him.   165

PORTIA You were to blame, I must be plain with you,
    To part so slightly with your wife's first gift,
    A thing stuck on with oaths upon your finger
    And so riveted with faith unto your flesh.
    I gave my love a ring, and made him swear   170
    Never to part with it, and here he stands.
    I dare be sworn for him he would not leave it
    Nor pluck it from his finger for the wealth
    That the world masters. Now in faith, Gratiano,
    You give your wife too unkind a cause of grief;   175
    And 'twere to me, I should be mad at it.

BASSANIO [*Aside*] Why, I were best to cut my left hand off
    And swear I lost the ring defending it.

GRATIANO My lord Bassanio gave his ring away
    Unto the judge that begged it, and indeed   180
    Deserved it too; and then the boy his clerk
    That took some pains in writing, he begged mine,
    And neither man nor master would take aught
    But the two rings.

PORTIA   What ring gave you, my lord?
    Not that, I hope, which you received of me?   185

BASSANIO If I could add a lie unto a fault,
    I would deny it; but you see my finger
    Hath not the ring upon it, it is gone.

PORTIA Even so void is your false heart of truth.
    By heaven, I will ne'er come in your bed   190
    Until I see the ring.

NERISSA   Nor I in yours
    Till I again see mine.

Portia and Bassanio spar over the missing ring. Bassanio insists that he gave it to the lawyer who saved Antonio's life. Portia declares that her revenge will be to deny this lawyer nothing.

1 A war of words (in pairs)

The first sequence of an elaborate verbal battle between Portia and Bassanio occurs in lines 192–208.

a Read the lines, emphasising the repetitions of 'ring'.
Read the lines again, concentrating not on fierce argument but on skirmishing with words. Try to use 'ring' differently each time you say it. Emphasise other repetitions and echoes that are used (the repeated rhythms of the lines are very strong). Who has the upper hand, Bassanio or Portia?

b Although the humorous interplay is usually entertaining in performance, it has occasionally been played with a degree of spite or torment, reinforcing the victory that Portia has so obviously won. Talk about this way of delivering the lines and the dramatic effects created. What atmosphere would you wish to create?

2 Is Portia like Shylock?

The 'rings' episode has uncanny echoes of the trial scene. Portia has trapped Bassanio by exploiting his inability to fulfil the terms of a bond. Like Shylock, she is utterly determined on her course of action.

Make a list of how alike and unalike Portia and Shylock are. Which do you think are more important: their similarities or their differences? Add to your list as you work through to the end of the play. Afterwards, you will find it helpful to compare your list with the discussion of the two characters on pages 171–4 and 177–8.

---

abate reduce
contain keep
What man ... ceremony? No man would have taken my love-gift ring if you had really explained its significance

civil doctor lawyer
held up defended
candles stars
liberal generous

BASSANIO   Sweet Portia,
　　　　If you did know to whom I gave the ring,
　　　　If you did know for whom I gave the ring,
　　　　And would conceive for what I gave the ring,   195
　　　　And how unwillingly I left the ring,
　　　　When naught would be accepted but the ring,
　　　　You would abate the strength of your displeasure.
PORTIA If you had known the virtue of the ring,
　　　　Or half her worthiness that gave the ring,   200
　　　　Or your own honour to contain the ring,
　　　　You would not then have parted with the ring.
　　　　What man is there so much unreasonable,
　　　　If you had pleased to have defended it
　　　　With any terms of zeal, wanted the modesty   205
　　　　To urge the thing held as a ceremony?
　　　　Nerissa teaches me what to believe:
　　　　I'll die for't, but some woman had the ring!
BASSANIO No by my honour, madam, by my soul
　　　　No woman had it, but a civil doctor,   210
　　　　Which did refuse three thousand ducats of me,
　　　　And begged the ring, the which I did deny him,
　　　　And suffered him to go displeased away,
　　　　Even he that had held up the very life
　　　　Of my dear friend. What should I say, sweet lady?   215
　　　　I was enforced to send it after him;
　　　　I was beset with shame and courtesy;
　　　　My honour would not let ingratitude
　　　　So much besmear it. Pardon me, good lady,
　　　　For by these blessèd candles of the night,   220
　　　　Had you been there I think you would have begged
　　　　The ring of me to give the worthy doctor.
PORTIA Let not that doctor e'er come near my house.
　　　　Since he hath got the jewel that I loved
　　　　And that which you did swear to keep for me,   225
　　　　I will become as liberal as you;
　　　　I'll not deny him anything I have,
　　　　No, not my body, nor my husband's bed:
　　　　Know him I shall, I am well sure of it.

Bassanio begs forgiveness, swearing always to be faithful. Portia mocks him; Antonio tries to help him. The rings are returned, but the teasing of Bassanio and Gratiano continues.

---

1 Is Bassanio grovelling? (in pairs)

Take it in turns to read aloud Bassanio's two speeches (lines 240–3 and 246–8). The first reader makes the words as oily and wheedling as possible. The second reader concentrates on being sincere and penitent. Which version works best?

2 Antonio to the rescue

In contrast to what happens at the trial, it is Antonio who speaks up for Bassanio (lines 249–53), swearing that his friend will always remain true to his word in the future ('nevermore break faith advisedly'). This time he pledges his soul as collateral.

Bassanio does not have time to reply before the rings plot moves towards its climax. But what does he think about his friend's new offer to be 'bound' on his behalf? Write a few lines for Bassanio in which you express your feelings about Antonio's selfless gesture.

3 'Are we cuckolds'? (in small groups)

Portia hands Bassanio's ring back, but her husband's relief at acquiring his ring is immediately undercut by Portia's assertion that she gained it from the lawyer in return for sleeping with him. Nerissa informs Gratiano that he too has been made a 'cuckold' (a man with an unfaithful wife). Talk together about the balance of comedy and seriousness that accompanies this taunting. Consider especially what might justify the two women taking their baiting of their husbands to such extremes.

Argus a monster with a hundred eyes
be well advised take care
mar . . . pen castrate him
double false
of credit to believe (meant ironically)
miscarried been lost

advisedly knowingly
lay/lie slept with
In lieu of in return for
cuckolds men with unfaithful wives
ere before

Lie not a night from home. Watch me like Argus.　　230
If you do not, if I be left alone,
Now by mine honour which is yet mine own,
I'll have that doctor for my bedfellow.

NERISSA And I his clerk; therefore be well advised
How you do leave me to mine own protection.　　235

GRATIANO Well, do you so. Let not me take him then,
For if I do, I'll mar the young clerk's pen.

ANTONIO I am th'unhappy subject of these quarrels.

PORTIA Sir, grieve not you; you are welcome notwithstanding.

BASSANIO Portia, forgive me this enforcèd wrong;　　240
And in the hearing of these many friends
I swear to thee, even by thine own fair eyes
Wherein I see myself –

PORTIA　　　　　　　　　　　Mark you but that?
In both my eyes he doubly sees himself:
In each eye one. Swear by your double self,　　245
And there's an oath of credit!

BASSANIO　　　　　　　　　　Nay, but hear me.
Pardon this fault, and by my soul I swear
I nevermore will break an oath with thee.

ANTONIO I once did lend my body for his wealth,
Which but for him that had your husband's ring　　250
Had quite miscarried. I dare be bound again,
My soul upon the forfeit, that your lord
Will nevermore break faith advisedly.

PORTIA Then you shall be his surety. Give him this,
And bid him keep it better than the other.　　255

ANTONIO Here, Lord Bassanio, swear to keep this ring.

BASSANIO By heaven, it is the same I gave the doctor!

PORTIA I had it of him; pardon me, Bassanio,
For by this ring the doctor lay with me.

NERISSA And pardon me, my gentle Gratiano,　　260
For that same scrubbèd boy the doctor's clerk,
In lieu of this, last night did lie with me.

GRATIANO Why, this is like the mending of highways
In summer where the ways are fair enough!
What, are we cuckolds ere we have deserved it?　　265

Portia reveals the truth about her deceptions and tells Antonio that three of his ships have been saved. Lorenzo and Jessica learn that Shylock will leave all his possessions to them.

---

1 All is revealed (in pairs)

One person reads Portia's lines 266–79. The other reacts as each character in turn. These unravellings (the **denouement**, or unknotting) of complex plots, when final disclosures are made, are a feature of many of Shakespeare's plays.

2 More letters!

Portia has two letters. One is from Bellario, explaining her part in the trial. The other is to Antonio (but from whom?), giving him good news about his ships. Choose one letter and write it.

3 'Strange accident' (in groups of three or four)

> You shall not know by what strange accident
> I chancèd on this letter.

Portia is very secretive about how she intercepted the letter giving good news to Antonio, and about when she got it. (If news of the argosies was received before the trial, the trial should not have happened and she made a fool of everyone.) Can you solve the mystery? After you have read to the end of the play, make up a short drama about how the letter fell into Portia's hands.

4 Shylock's legacy

Nerissa's final words tell us that Shylock has committed himself by 'deed of gift' to leave all his wealth to Lorenzo and Jessica when he dies. Once again, he is un-named, referred to only as 'the rich Jew'. Reproduce the actual document which Nerissa hands to Lorenzo.

---

soon quickly
road anchor in harbour
manna heavenly food

charge . . . inter'gatories be examined under oath

PORTIA Speak not so grossly; you are all amazed.
        Here is a letter, read it at your leisure;
        It comes from Padua, from Bellario.
        There you shall find that Portia was the doctor,
        Nerissa there her clerk. Lorenzo here   270
        Shall witness I set forth as soon as you,
        And even but now returned; I have not yet
        Entered my house. Antonio, you are welcome;
        And I have better news in store for you
        Than you expect. Unseal this letter soon;   275
        There you shall find three of your argosies
        Are richly come to harbour suddenly.
        You shall not know by what strange accident
        I chancèd on this letter.
ANTONIO   I am dumb.
BASSANIO Were you the doctor and I knew you not?   280
GRATIANO Were you the clerk that is to make me cuckold?
NERISSA Ay, but the clerk that never means to do it,
        Unless he live until he be a man.
BASSANIO Sweet doctor, you shall be my bedfellow;
        When I am absent, then lie with my wife.   285
ANTONIO Sweet lady, you have given me life and living;
        For here I read for certain that my ships
        Are safely come to road.
PORTIA   How now, Lorenzo?
        My clerk hath some good comforts too for you.
NERISSA Ay, and I'll give them him without a fee.   290
        There do I give to you and Jessica
        From the rich Jew, a special deed of gift
        After his death of all he dies possessed of.
LORENZO Fair ladies, you drop manna in the way
        Of starvèd people.
PORTIA   It is almost morning;   295
        And yet I am sure you are not satisfied
        Of these events at full. Let us go in,
        And charge us there upon inter'gatories,
        And we will answer all things faithfully.

It is almost dawn as the characters go into Portia's house. Gratiano looks forward to going to bed with Nerissa, determined never again to relinquish her ring!

---

1 Questions . . .

As the characters prepare to leave the stage, Portia uses the language of the courtroom as she promises to 'answer all things faithfully'. Make up a question that each character in the play wishes to ask her about what has been going on.

2 Gratiano has the last word (in pairs)

a Gratiano's final line not only puns on the word 'ring' (which also meant 'female genitals' to the Elizabethans) but also reminds the audience of the need to protect and value love tokens. Talk about what you think of ending the play in this way.

b Step into role as Shakespeare. Choose a different character to end the play, and write their speech.

c Read again what each character says in their final lines. Talk about whether you think the speeches reveal something important about each character. Jessica is silent. What is she thinking?

3 Curtain! Lights fade (in groups of any size)

Don't forget Shylock! The 2004 film ended with Shylock excluded from the ghetto (see p. 168) and Jessica gazing out of a window. A stage production ended with Shylock at prayer after Gratiano's speech. Another had Jessica left alone and desolate on stage as all the Christians had gone off, ignoring her. What final impression would you wish to create? Present a tableau of the final moment of your own production.

---

inter'gatory question   **sore** much

GRATIANO Let it be so. The first inter'gatory   300
      That my Nerissa shall be sworn on is:
      Whether till the next night she had rather stay,
      Or go to bed now, being two hours to day.
      But were the day come, I should wish it dark,
      Till I were couching with the doctor's clerk.   305
      Well, while I live I'll fear no other thing
      So sore as keeping safe Nerissa's ring.

                                      Exeunt

FINIS

Looking back at the play
Activities for groups or individuals

---

1 To cut or not to cut . . .

Some critics have argued that the play would retain its dramatic integrity if it ended with the conclusion of the trial scene in Act 4, with Shylock defeated and Antonio saved. But it is evident that Shakespeare is concerned to continue to explore themes that have preoccupied the drama of the first four acts, even though his intention might be to promote comedy rather than deadly seriousness.

a Look back at the single scene that comprises Act 5. Head up three columns with 'Appearance versus reality'; 'Justice versus mercy'; 'Love versus hate'. Record all the examples of each theme that you can find in Act 5.

b Compare the different dramatic effects created in Acts 4 and 5 by the themes listed in Activity 1a above.

c If you were directing the play, would you include Act 5 or would you cut it altogether and end the play at the close of the trial scene?

2 Morning has broken . . .

Look back through Act 5. Pick out words and phrases that show day gradually breaking. Talk together about why the act begins in moonlight and darkness and ends with daylight.

3 Antonio's sadness

Just as Antonio's sadness haunts the opening of the play, many productions tend to focus on his isolation and loneliness at the end of the play (see p. 176 and picture at bottom of p. xii). Although his life has been saved and his finances restored, his sadness seems unresolved. Write entries for his diary which capture his thoughts and feelings at the close of the play.

4 Happy ever after?

Act 5 focuses on three married couples:

Portia and Bassanio

Nerissa and Gratiano

Jessica and Lorenzo

Will the marriages last? What do you think?

5 Ten years on . . . an interview with Shylock

Shylock does not appear in Act 5. There is only news that he has willed his remaining wealth to Jessica and Lorenzo. Imagine that you are a researcher for a magazine. One of your tasks is to track down and interview Shylock ten years after the point at which the play ends, and to find out how his life has changed. Conduct the interview.

6 Bassanio and Portia

a Choose a line from Act 5 which you think fits this photograph of Bassanio and Portia.

b Compare this production's choice of historical setting with that pictured on page 143.

What is the play about?

The Merchant of Venice has fascinated and intrigued audiences and critics ever since Shakespeare wrote it some time around 1597. Although it brilliantly fuses together a host of dramatic elements and at least four separate narrative strands, the play has become best known for the character Shylock and the relentless pursuit of his bond. Shylock appears in only five of the twenty scenes, but his presence dominates the play.

Prior to the nineteenth century, Shylock was played as a grotesque stage villain. Since then, his character has been portrayed as more complex. Most directors have sought to present him as a more sympathetic and vulnerable character whose moving plea for the common humanity of all races has become central to interpretations: 'Hath not a Jew eyes?' (Act 3 Scene 1, line 46).

One way of answering the question 'What is *The Merchant of Venice* about?' is to think of it as the dramatic weaving together of four stories:

- the bond: Shylock and the pound of flesh
- the caskets: the winning of Portia
- the elopement: Jessica and Lorenzo
- the rings: a love test.

None of these strands was Shakespeare's own invention. The 'bond' and 'rings' narratives were probably based on a contemporary Italian short story, the tale of Gianetto of Venice and the lady of Belmont. The collection of short stories from which it was taken was called *Il Pecorone* (The Idiot). Shakespeare drew on this source but made it more dramatic. In the original, it is the hero's godfather who is to be punished by losing a pound of flesh. Shakespeare also makes the device of the rings more comic by adding the parallel story of Gratiano and Nerissa. The 'caskets' and 'elopement' narratives were drawn from well-known traditional stories that were part of the popular culture of Shakespeare's time. Again, he gave them new dramatic life; for example, in the play's version of the 'caskets' story, not only is Portia restricted by her dead father's will, but she also receives three different suitors, rather than the same one three times as in the original tale.

◆ Look back at the play and place the four strands in ascending order of importance, as you see them. Write a paragraph about each strand saying what the play would lose or gain if it were omitted.

Themes in *The Merchant of Venice*

Another way of looking at the play is to discuss its themes. Themes are ideas or issues or topics which recur throughout the play (rather like repeated melodies in a piece of music). They suggest that Shakespeare was preoccupied by particular ideas as he wrote, and sought to explore them through drama that would entertain his audiences – and make them think! Such major themes include: love versus hate, appearance versus reality, Venice versus Belmont, justice versus mercy, comedy versus tragedy, trade versus usury, fathers versus daughters, Christian versus Jew (which is explored in 'History and the Jews', pp. 186–8).

Love versus hate

On the one hand, the play is full of love and friendship. Bassanio's courtship of Portia is romantic and passionate. Portia is a woman in love, desperate to give herself to the man she desires. She speaks of 'ecstasy' and 'joy'. Bassanio praises Portia as a 'demi-god' with 'sugar breath'. Gratiano and Nerissa fall in love at first sight. 'Lorenzo and his amorous Jessica' are two young lovers who elope romantically. Antonio and Bassanio seem to share a deep, homoerotic closeness. Solanio says of Antonio: 'I think he only loves the world for him [Bassanio]'. It is, at the very least, a 'true friendship' which prompts Antonio to great self-sacrifice.

On the other hand, bitterness and hatred are constantly evident. Portia is overtly racist in dismissing her suitors ('Let all of his complexion choose me so'). Virtually all characters express racist comments at some point in the play. Lancelot and Gratiano openly revile Shylock, Lancelot comparing Shylock's Jewishness with 'the devil'. Hatred is expressed through verbal insults against him, many of which take his name away from him (see p. 188). Shylock turns his hatred of Christians ('I hate him [Antonio] for he is a Christian') into revenge on his Christian tormentors. Jessica, Shylock's only child, hates the strictures of home and smears his name as well as plundering his possessions.

◆ Make a drawing of a pair of scales. Place expressions of love and friendship on the side of one scale, and expressions of hate on the other. Use your findings to help you write a short essay about the ways in which the play explores the presentation of love versus hate.

Appearance versus reality: 'All that glisters is not gold'

The Merchant of Venice shows the danger of valuing only what can be seen on the surface. When Antonio calls Shylock 'a villain with a smiling cheek' he hints at the dark intentions that lie behind Shylock's apparent beneficence. Rich and successful Venice contains prejudice at all levels. Behind Portia's 'fair' exterior and politeness there lurks nasty racism. The caskets of gold and silver disguise secrets which contradict their outward appearance. Gratiano must hide his natural boisterousness in order to accompany Bassanio to Belmont. Lancelot cruelly deceives his father, as does Jessica hers, but with more devastating effect. She also disguises her womanhood in male garments in order to escape Shylock's control. Similarly, Portia and Nerissa adopt male disguises to challenge the men in the courtroom. The device of the rings explores the issue of betrayal, besides adding to the confusion of identities. Characters frequently mislead or deceive each other.

◆ Working in a small group, make a list of the main characters. Write alongside each the various deceptions they practise. Then prepare a presentation to other groups on the theme of appearance versus reality in *The Merchant of Venice*.

Venice versus Belmont

To Shakespeare's contemporaries, Venice was a legendary city of prosperity, sophistication and culture. It was a world-famous centre for banking and trade and, like England in the 1590s, promoted the ventures and interests of its powerful merchants, whilst still protecting the established social privileges of its aristocracy. Venice was also renowned for its tolerance of foreigners, founded upon a legal system that protected the rights of all individuals, not only its own citizens. However, it confined its Jewish inhabitants to their own neighbourhood – the ghetto.

Belmont (literally 'fair mountain') does not actually exist. It is Shakespeare's own imaginative creation, based on an idea he took from his source material. Belmont seems to reflect the Elizabethan ideal of the country estate, resonating with artistic, musical and cultural assurance. It appears to be a place of beauty and elegance, presided over by an intelligent and gracious mistress. But is it so different from Venice? In spite of its charm, it is riddled with patriarchal control and intolerance of foreigners.

- ◆ Choose a scene which you think typically represents Venetian values and principles. Do the same for Belmont. Write an analysis of the similarities and differences of the two settings used by Shakespeare.

Justice versus mercy

One of the central preoccupations of the play is justice: the right, proper and fair treatment of individuals according to their deserts. The conflict between justice and mercy is most dramatically explored in the trial scene, where the trial of Antonio turns into the trial of Shylock. Although he is constantly requested to show mercy to the accused Antonio, Shylock refuses. Portia's moving declaration in her speech that begins 'The quality of mercy is not strained' summarises the argument that justice is most appropriately done when mercy tempers it. At the end of the trial, both the Duke and Antonio boast of their merciful attitude. Shylock receives judgement, but does he receive justice?

- ◆ In a group, talk together about the trial scene. Which characters display mercy, and how?

Comedy versus tragedy

The play seems to end on a happy note, with the resolution of the test of the rings and the celebration of marriage. But even though the final act tracks the symbolic movement from night to dawn and is set in Belmont, there are many darker aspects which cast shadows over that bright ending. Shylock leaves the court a broken man, crushed by the instruction that he must convert to Christianity. In many productions, Antonio stands alone among the pairs of married couples at the end of the play, his sadness unresolved. In others, Jessica is shunned and ostracised in Belmont. Lancelot treats his blind father with apparent disdain. Shylock is constantly reviled and baited by Christian characters delighting at his misfortune and mocking his losses.

- ◆ Compile lists of the comic and tragic elements in *The Merchant of Venice*. Use your findings as the basis of a five-minute presentation discussing how you would direct the play to bring out both its comic and tragic aspects.

Trade versus usury

Shylock, as a typical Jewish merchant, practises usury: the lending of money and charging interest on its repayment. To him, making money from money is legitimate business and an art at which he is skilled. 'I make it breed as fast', Shylock proudly boasts to Antonio, comparing his own generation of profit with the ingenuity of the biblical figure of Jacob. The play also shows that money-lending is one of the only ways in which Jews were allowed to earn a living and Shylock is critical of Christians who 'lend out money gratis' (without charging interest). But Christianity forbade the charging of interest and Antonio scornfully challenges Shylock's practice: 'I neither lend nor borrow / By taking nor by giving of excess'. The Christians condemn usurers but, hypocritically, depend on the money of the Jews to underwrite their own economic projects. Bassanio has frittered away his wealth but is quite prepared to use Shylock's lending service to support his courtship of Portia, seeing it very much as a business venture.

◆ Find examples in the play of the differing attitudes towards usury displayed by Christian and Jew. Then research present attitudes to usury. Is it still considered wrong in some societies?

Fathers versus daughters

Both Portia and Jessica struggle to come to terms with the demands made on them by their fathers. Shakespeare gives little information about Portia's father, but he controls her destiny from beyond the grave ('so is the will of a living daughter curbed by the will of a dead father'), insisting that her choice of husband is dictated by the lottery of the caskets. Jessica is uncomfortable at home ('Our house is hell') and speaks of being 'ashamed' to be Shylock's daughter. She is clearly unhappy with the tediousness of her domestic life and plans to elope with the Christian Lorenzo as a way of escape.

◆ Although Portia's father was a Christian and lived in Belmont and Shylock is Jewish and lives in Venice, do they share any common attitudes towards fatherhood and to their daughters? Talk about this with a partner and then give a short presentation to the class on your observations.

Characters

Shylock: villain or victim?

The age-old dilemma about Shylock is this: is he tragic or is he comic? And, of course, he's both. He's one of the most complex human beings Shakespeare wrote.   *Sir Peter Hall, theatre director*

He becomes that which he most abhors. He's torn to shreds emotionally by the society around him. He becomes the very thing that's reduced him . . . that's taken his humanity away.

Dustin Hoffman, actor

If the audience can love him and hate him, understand him, then not understand him . . . then you've got him.   *Henry Goodman, actor*

There has always been controversy about Shylock. To some he is a miserly money-lender who delights in the prospect of cutting a pound of flesh from the noble merchant who has exposed his corrupt ways. He is a bloodthirsty fiend armed with scales and a knife, who cares more for his money than for his runaway daughter. Such a view sees him as a comic or malign villain who gets his comeuppance in the end.

A quite different perspective sees him as the victim of the society around him. Here he is a godly, clean-living family man who merely wishes to conduct his business unimpeded. He becomes a man driven to revenge by mindless persecution and the cruel theft of his only child. This view casts him as a naive, misguided soul who tries to get even within the law of those who hate him, only to be cruelly tricked and humiliated yet again.

There's no simple answer to the question 'villain or victim?', but the fact that Shylock has fascinated audiences for 400 years is evidence that he is one of Shakespeare's most human and believable characters. What follows will help you to form your own view of Shylock, although you will detect a strongly anti-racist stance in what we, the editors of this edition, have written. No one can be neutral about *The Merchant of Venice*.

Shylock and the Christians

Shylock's trouble with the Christians dates back to well before the start of the play. He speaks of an 'ancient grudge' when he first appears, and gives a vivid account of Antonio's racist bullying.

◆ Read lines 98–121 of Act 1 Scene 3 and make a full list of Antonio's insults and abuses against Shylock.

Despite the enmity between Antonio and Shylock, the Christian still does business with the Jew. Antonio is fully aware of the ominous terms of the bond which he signs in the presence of a lawyer. Shylock makes no secret of his intentions if his enemy can't pay up at the end of three months. Then the unthinkable happens: Antonio loses all his ships, and with them his wealth. He is not only bankrupt but also trapped by his bond with the Jew. Antonio entered willingly into the deal to help Bassanio, knowing full well what the consequences might be. Nevertheless, the Christians are outraged when Shylock claims what is lawfully his.

◆ Collect quotations which show Christian objections to Shylock's bond before Portia intervenes.

Shylock might be accused of wishing to trap Antonio, but the Christians similarly conspire against him. They invite him to dinner on the very night a gang of them help Lorenzo steal Jessica, along with a considerable portion of his wealth. Portia also carefully plans her action against Shylock. In the trial, she waits until the very moment he is going to cut Antonio's flesh to reveal the loophole she has discovered in the bond between them. Before that, she repeatedly gives Shylock the chance to back down, so adding to the humiliation she clearly wishes to inflict on him in her hour of victory. When Shylock is defeated, he is shown little of the mercy which before was so earnestly recommended to him by Portia. Half his wealth is confiscated and – far worse – he must lose his faith and convert to Christianity.

◆ As Portia, write your own account of your involvement in the trial. Explain your plan to rescue Antonio and defeat Shylock. Why did you show him no mercy?

How Shylock responds to prejudice

Shylock's bloodthirsty campaign against Antonio is morally indefensible. He eschews the simple purity of his normal life and degrades himself in his animal-like quest to win a pound of the Christian's flesh. His behaviour is wrong, but it is understandable. Shylock is a foreigner in his own city. He may have lived all his life in Venice, yet he is treated as an alien. Like his fellow Jews, he tries to rise above such prejudice and seeks security and success in money-lending, which he calls 'well won thrift'; Antonio disparagingly calls it 'interest'. Antonio and the Christians won't allow themselves to lend money for profit, but to support their extravagant lifestyles they still need money loans from the Jews they persecute. Shylock has been waiting to strike back at Antonio, one of Venice's principal anti–Semites, and sees his chance when the merchant is compelled to come to him for credit.

Significantly, Shylock tries to attack his enemy within the law of Venice. He is often at pains to point out the legality of his actions, and after the loss of Antonio's ships refers obsessively and repeatedly to his 'bond'. In the trial, he openly questions the validity of Venetian justice if it is not to be enforced on his behalf. He demands that his case is dealt with according to the letter of the law, and of course this is turned harshly against him when it is revealed that he himself has behaved illegally.

◆ Collect Shylock's references to his legal agreement with Antonio and other comments he makes about the law. Use your findings to write several paragraphs about why it is so important to Shylock to be able to use the law of Venice against Antonio.

Shylock despises Antonio from the start of the play. His hatred is intensified by the loss of Jessica, perhaps the key to his emotional reactions from then on. In his clash with Salarino and Solanio just after Jessica's elopement (Act 3 Scene 1) he claims that his suffering and anger are produced by the Christians themselves. He blames his villainy on them, arguing that it is simply imitation of their own prejudice and cruelty.

◆ Reread lines 42–57 of Act 3 Scene 1. How convinced are you of Shylock's justification for his actions? Think of actual examples in history or modern times which show that racism provokes similar cruelty in its victims.

Was Shakespeare anti-Semitic in his depiction of Shylock?

Shakespeare's characters, notably in *The Merchant of Venice*, often express racist views, but whether Shakespeare himself was a racist is open to dispute. What is clear is that he understood the suffering and the behaviour which results from racial prejudice. Shylock's key speech in Act 3 Scene 1 is a plea of supreme eloquence for our common humanity. However, Shakespeare's handling of Shylock is deeply ambiguous. Shylock is intensely and movingly human, yet at the end he receives the same treatment as a stage villain. He leaves the court in Act 4 with hardly a word, apparently completely defeated. One would have thought that Shakespeare wouldn't want us to forget about him, but he doesn't appear in Act 5 and is barely mentioned there. If Shakespeare wanted the audience to view this central character as a victim, surely he'd give him something to say or do in the final act?

◆ Your school or college drama group wishes to stage *The Merchant of Venice*, but is opposed by the head or principal, who fears that the play might offend ethnic minority groups in the school and the local community. The head calls a meeting for those involved. Decide who would be present and improvise this difficult encounter in front of the rest of the class. Everyone, including those observing, has the right to stop the action to ask questions, to express opinions, and to ask for or offer advice.

Shylock's changing portrayal

In the early days of English theatre, Shylock was performed to match the way he is described by his Christian enemies. He was presented as a comic villain, grotesque, outrageously caricatured as the miserly money-lender. He later became evil and terrifying, a villain who was incapable of humour and who was stubborn, malicious and threatening. In the nineteenth century, Edmund Kean broke away from this widely accepted view by portraying him as an intelligent and vulnerable character whose dignity and isolation made him increasingly sympathetic. Shylock's pleas for humanity and understanding became central in performance. Emphasis on his 'Hath not a Jew eyes?' speech softened the harshness and repellence which had earlier characterised him. This changed him from a comic character to much more of a tragic one. He became less of a villain, more of a victim, whose hatred and desire for revenge exposed the injustice and intolerance of the society in which he lived.

More recent critical character studies have explored his usury and his Jewish background more fully and placed his Jewishness at the heart of his conflict with the Christians. He is widely viewed as a foreigner, an outsider, even an alien within the social context of the play. He is seen as vital to the play's exploration of religious and cultural identity, and is central to the play's moral impact.

◆ Try to arrange the opposite sequence of photographs of past Shylocks in chronological order. What do these images suggest about how these different actors portrayed him?

◆ In your own production, how would you want Shylock to be played? As the director, write some notes for other members of the company, justifying your ideas. Include a sketch of an appropriate costume design.

Antonio and the Christians

Venice is almost completely characterised by friendships between men. The Christians are 'friends' but are largely a band of merchants and traders bound together by a group identity. They oppose the Jews and the Jewish practice of usury. They profit from trade. The Venetians are competitive and commercially driven, conscious of status and hierarchy, although they seem to have idle hours to spend.

Antonio

Antonio is the merchant of the play's title (although an eighteenth-century version of the play renamed it *The Jew of Venice*). Traditionally, he has been seen as an affluent gentleman, at ease within refined social and economic circles, very much associated with the values and attitudes represented by Venice. Antonio is generous to Bassanio but loathes Shylock. The reason for his sadness at the start of the play is left unresolved, although in many modern productions his loneliness and sadness have been attributed to homoerotic feelings for Bassanio. He is quite willing to die under Shylock's knife as long as he can see Bassanio one last time. Some productions ensure that he is left isolated at the end of the play as the married couples celebrate.

Bassanio

Like the other male Christian characters, Bassanio belongs to a wealthy, privileged class in Venice, but as a result of his reckless spending he is impoverished as the play opens. He conforms to the Elizabethan model of a gentleman as 'a scholar and a soldier'. He might love and desire Portia, but he also views marriage to her as a business opportunity and he quickly assumes the role as head of Belmont. His friendship for Antonio is strong (Antonio is 'The dearest friend to me, the kindest man' and a 'true friend'), powerful enough to postpone his marriage to Portia as Antonio nears his trial. But Bassanio is passionately attracted to Portia, whom he describes in heightened, romantic terms as: 'fair, and – fairer than that word – / Of wondrous virtues' and a 'demi-god'.

Gratiano, Solanio and Salarino

These three men are united not only by their friendship but by their violent hostility towards Shylock. Gratiano's withering attacks peak during the trial scene. Solanio and Salarino gloat over Shylock's loss of his daughter and his jewels, then taunt him publicly and excruciatingly about Jessica's elopement.

Women in Venice and Belmont

Venice is ruled entirely by men. Women have no role at all in trade, politics or law. It seems that they cannot even own property. As soon as Portia enters Venetian society by becoming engaged to Bassanio, she gives him all her wealth as well as her own freedom:

> This house, these servants, and this same myself
> Are yours, my lord's.   *Act 3 Scene 2, lines 170–1*

Patriarchy rules in Belmont as well as Venice. Portia might be head of the household at the start of the play, but her father still controls her destiny, even from the grave. When she escapes from her father's will, she subjects herself immediately to her husband's authority. From now on she will be known as 'Lord Bassanio's wife' rather than Portia.

◆ Read through the scenes in Acts 1–3 in which women appear. Make a list of all the ways in which their lives are restricted.
◆ Turn to the cast list on page 1. Rank each character in order of social status as perceived by a) the Duke, b) Jessica, c) yourself.

The three women in the play have very different personalities. None the less, they all marry friends of Antonio at roughly the same time and are all involved in the defeat of Shylock. All adopt disguises as men in order to effect that defeat. Both Portia and Jessica are victims of their fathers' patriarchal authority and control. Portia may not marry freely. Jessica, perhaps frustrated by her father's over–protectiveness, decides to convert to Christianity.

◆ Study the pen portraits that follow. Check how far you agree with each, then write a short essay of your own on each of the women, or attempt the activity that follows each portrait.

Portia

Most criticism points to the inconsistencies in Portia's presentation. She has many seemingly paradoxical identities:

- the dutiful daughter, compliant to her dead father's will
- the innocent young woman ('unlessoned . . . unschooled, unpractised')
- the 'mortal-breathing saint' who possesses 'god–like amity'
- the hard-headed and calculating lawyer who is fully conversant with the tricks of the legal trade
- the advocate of mercy who ruthlessly destroys Shylock

- the innocent virgin who knows all about male sexuality
- the racist mocker of the suitors she finds unfavourable
- the wealthy and independent woman who nevertheless gives herself willingly to her husband's authority
- the mocking, teasing and barbed tormentor of her husband in the 'rings' test.

Key questions arise when thinking about Portia. Is she an innocent, virtuous heroine or a devious manipulator who subverts the meaning of what she says? Is she fundamental to the preservation of the male values and attitudes of Venice and Belmont or does she stand for female resistance in a male world, taking on and defeating men at their own game? Will being subservient to a man like Bassanio suit Portia?

◆ Study the two pictures below. Talk together about how they reveal different aspects of Portia's character. Then write a short essay on the complexities of the way that Shakespeare presents Portia.

Jessica

Jessica is ashamed to be Shylock's daughter and views her life at home as 'hell'. Only the joking of Lancelot relieves the domestic gloom. She is perhaps frustrated by her father's over-protectiveness and killjoy attitude. She willingly becomes involved in a Christian plot and schemes against her father behind his back. She plunders from him much of his money and jewels, including a turquoise ring of great sentimental value, which later she is alleged to have squandered. In order to elope with Lorenzo, she dons the disguise of a man. On arriving at Belmont she is apparently shunned by the Christians whose religion she will soon embrace.

Questions that arise when considering Jessica include: does she willingly condemn her father's pursuit of revenge in Act 3 Scene 2, or does she seek to ingratiate herself with her Christian hosts? Is she really a huge admirer of Portia (as she claims in Act 3 Scene 5, lines 63–71) or does she have little reason to like or respect her? How will she fare married to Lorenzo, whom she teasingly accuses of 'Stealing her soul with many vows of faith, / And ne'er a true one'?

◆ Imagine you are a journalist for a women's magazine. It is now ten years after the play ends. For a 'Where Are They Now?' feature you decide to trace and interview Jessica. Write your article, giving details of how she feels about the events of the decade before, and how her life has changed since then.

Nerissa

Nerissa is more than a servant to Portia; she is almost a lady-in-waiting or confidante (see picture on p. vi). Portia trusts her completely and she takes orders from Portia without question. Nerissa has common sense and a practical approach to life, displaying humour and worldly wisdom in her attitude to Portia's suitors and to men in general.

In spite of the fact that she has no illusions about men, why does she fall for Gratiano? She can identify that Bassanio 'was the best deserving a fair lady' but apparently ignores the fact that her own husband is a show-off and a racist bully. After watching the lengthy, ritualistic courtship of Portia, why does she agree to Gratiano after knowing him such a very short time? How will she cope with such a husband?

◆ Nerissa volunteers to be interviewed for a local radio feature on 'Life at Belmont'. Script her contribution, making clear her attitudes to her life with her mistress and her new husband.

The language of *The Merchant of Venice*

Imagery

The Merchant of Venice abounds in imagery: vivid words and phrases that help create the atmosphere of the play as they conjure up emotionally charged pictures or associations in the mind. When Portia describes the concept of 'mercy', she declares that 'It droppeth as the gentle rain from heaven', bestowing heaven's blessing on giver and receiver alike. Similarly, Antonio voices his mistrust of Shylock and his motives in agreeing to the 'bond' by calling him 'a villain with a smiling cheek', outwardly benign but inwardly malevolent.

Imagery carries powerful significance, far deeper than its surface meaning. Images enrich particular moments. When Shylock strengthens his determination to seek revenge on the Christians who have persecuted him, he twists one of the insults used against him back on his tormentors: 'Thou call'dst me dog before thou hadst a cause, / But since I am a dog, beware my fangs.' Imagery repeatedly illuminates the themes of the play, such as love and deception (as when Portia doubts the veracity of Bassanio's love words by suggesting that he is being tortured 'upon the rack / Where men enforcèd do speak anything').

Imagery gives pleasure as it stirs the audience's imagination and deepens the impact of particular moments or moods. It provides insight into character, and intensifies meaning and emotional force. In *The Merchant of Venice* the imagery is sometimes so highly embroidered and extravagant that it seems full of **hyperbole** (exaggeration). Bassanio's praise of Portia's picture, which he finds in the lead casket, is often judged as showy and ornamental, perhaps reflecting his posturing and insincerity:

> Here are severed lips
> Parted with sugar breath; so sweet a bar
> Should sunder such sweet friends. Here in her hairs
> The painter plays the spider, and hath woven
> A golden mesh t'entrap the hearts of men   *Act 3 Scene 2, lines 118–22*

Shakespeare's imagery uses metaphor, simile or personification. All are comparisons which in effect substitute one thing (the image) for another (the thing described).

A **simile** compares one thing to another using 'like' or 'as'. Shylock contemptuously describes Antonio as looking 'like a fawning publican'. Arragon, ironically, declares that the fool who chooses by outward show is 'like the martlet [swift]' building its nest on an exposed outer wall, vulnerable to danger and misfortune.

A **metaphor** is also a comparison, suggesting that two dissimilar things are actually the same. When Arragon leaves, Portia judges: 'Thus hath the candle singed the moth.' Arragon ('the moth') has been emotionally wounded ('singed') in his unsuccessful attempt to win Portia and her wealth, signified by the silver casket ('the candle') which has so attracted him.

Personification turns all kinds of things into persons, giving them human feelings or attributes. Lorenzo personifies the attractive qualities of the night: 'How sweet the moonlight sleeps upon this bank!' Portia acknowledges the radiant power of light: 'How far that little candle throws his beams!' Jessica insists that 'love is blind'.

Certain image clusters recur through the play, notably those of classical mythology, and love and hate.

Classical mythology Bassanio's pursuit of Portia is compared to Jason's seeking the Golden Fleece at 'Colchos' strand'. Gratiano relates his and Bassanio's success at Belmont to that of the great heroic adventurer: 'We are the Jasons, we have won the fleece'. Portia is a worthy prize, likened to 'Cato's daughter, Brutus' Portia'. Portia's reputation is further strengthened when Shakespeare compares her to the revered prophetess Sibylla and to the goddess of chastity, Diana. Portia sees Bassanio as the heroic warrior Hercules, who rescued Hesione (a sacrificial virgin) from a threatening sea monster. In the final act, Shakespeare draws on a list of doomed romantic partnerships to create an ominous mood: Troilus and Cressida, Thisbe and Pyramus, Dido and Aeneas, Medea and Aeson.

Love Images of different types of love abound. Portia, anxious that Bassanio might choose incorrectly, predicts 'my eye shall be the stream / And watery deathbed for him'. But when he chooses the lead casket, she declares 'In measure rain thy joy'. To Bassanio, Portia is a 'demi-god' whose hair 'hath woven / A golden mesh t'entrap the hearts of men'. Morocco describes her as 'this shrine, this mortal breathing saint'. Lorenzo finds Jessica to be 'sweet, / Even in the lovely garnish of a boy'. Shakespeare also uses images to define character. Gratiano's expressions of love are, typically, coarsely sexual, as when he includes the phrase 'stake down' (with a limp penis) as he bets with Bassanio on who will have the first son.

Hate Lancelot compares Shylock's Jewishness with 'the devil'. Verbal insults against Shylock include 'cut-throat dog', 'stranger cur', 'dog Jew' and 'wolf' (see p. 188). Jessica hates her home: 'Our house is hell'. Shylock detests Christian entertainment: 'fools with varnished faces'. He turns his hatred back on his Christian tormentors: 'If I can catch him once upon the hip, / I will feed fat the ancient grudge I bear him.'

◆ Identify a dozen striking and powerful images in the play. Draw them in a bold, visual way that explores the comparisons at the heart of each one.

Antithesis

Antithesis is the opposition of words or phrases against each other, as in Portia's command to Antonio in the trial scene: 'You must prepare your bosom for his knife'. This setting of word against word ('your bosom' stands in vulnerable contrast to the menace of 'his knife') is one of Shakespeare's favourite language devices. He uses it extensively in all his plays. Why? Because antithesis powerfully expresses conflict through its use of opposites, and conflict is the essence of all drama. In *The Merchant of Venice*, conflict occurs in many forms: Christian versus Jew, mercy versus justice, father versus daughter, usury versus trade, appearance versus reality (see pp. 167–70). Antithesis intensifies that sense of conflict.

In Lancelot's first appearance, his soliloquy shows him struggling to weigh the arguments of 'fiend' versus 'conscience': should he run away from Shylock's service, or stay? '"Budge!" says the fiend. "Budge not!" says my conscience' (Act 2 Scene 2, lines 14–15).

Antonio's description of Shylock (Act 1 Scene 3, lines 90–4) bristles with antitheses. As he questions Shylock's integrity, he sets 'devil' against 'Scripture', 'evil soul' against 'holy witness' and so on. The same theme of false appearance is explored in a long series of antitheses by Bassanio as he contemplates making his choice of caskets (Act 3 Scene 2, lines 73–107). He considers in turn law, religion, cowardice, courage and beauty, showing how vice can be hidden beneath a mask of virtue:

There is no vice so simple but assumes /
Some mark of virtue on his outward parts.   *Act 3 Scene 2, lines 81–2*

In Act 3 Scene 1, where Shylock makes his plea for common humanity and considers his revenge, the differences between Christian and Jew are powerfully expressed: 'amen' and 'prayer' pivot against 'devil' (line 17). Shylock antithetically sets all he holds dear against Antonio's reaction: 'laughed' against 'losses'; 'mocked' against 'gains'; 'scorned' against 'nation'; 'cooled my friends' against 'heated mine enemies' (lines 43–5).

◆ Collect about twenty examples of antithesis. Use them in an extended essay showing how antithesis helps create a sense of conflict in *The Merchant of Venice*.

Verse and prose

About 80 per cent of the play is in verse, 20 per cent is in prose. How did Shakespeare decide whether to write in verse or prose? One answer is that he followed theatrical convention. Prose was traditionally used by comic and low-status characters. High-status characters spoke verse. Comic scenes were written in prose (as were letters, like Bellario's), but audiences expected verse in serious scenes: the poetic style was thought to be particularly suitable for moments of high dramatic or emotional intensity, and for tragic themes.

Many of the Christians in the play are wealthy and educated, so they speak mainly in verse. Just as their clothes are richly elaborate, their language is similarly extravagant or high-flown. Salarino's ships would 'Enrobe the roaring waters with my silks'.

Lancelot (low-status) uses prose consistently. He and Old Gobbo, his father, represent the poor and uneducated in the play. Lancelot's language is usually comic and fast-moving. Old Gobbo refers constantly to his Christian faith – much more so than his social superiors. With these characters, Shakespeare sticks rigidly to the language rules for social class.

But both Portia (very high-status) and Nerissa speak all of Act 1 Scene 2 in prose, perhaps because Shakespeare considered it a comic scene. Similarly, Lorenzo (high-status) speaks prose in his dialogue with Lancelot in Act 3 Scene 5, as does Jessica (but they revert to verse when speaking to each other). Shylock, as a Jew, has low status in Venice, and many of his speeches are in prose. The fact that his 'Hath not a Jew eyes?' speech is in prose demonstrates that Shakespeare can use prose just as effectively as verse to express the deepest feelings and the most profound thoughts. None the less, in the trial scene Shylock consistently uses verse, perhaps because the scene is serious, and he is in the company of high-status characters.

The verse of *The Merchant of Venice* is mainly blank verse: unrhymed verse written in iambic pentameter. It usually has ten syllables per line, and each line has five beats or 'stresses'. This line of Portia's is marked to show the stressed (/) and unstressed (×) syllables:

```
×  /   ×   /   ×  / ×  / ×   /
```
Behold, there stand the caskets, noble prince.

◆ Read the line aloud in unison with your partner, but pronounce each syllable very clearly, almost as if each one were a separate word. As you read, beat out the five-stress rhythm (e.g. clap hands, tap the desk).

◆ Now turn to lines 33–7 in Act 1 Scene 3. Repeat what you have just done. Can you find the rhythm? When you have found it, try the exercise again with verse spoken by another character. The choice is yours!

By the time Shakespeare wrote *The Merchant of Venice*, he was becoming more flexible and experimental in his use of iambic pentameter. End-stopped lines are less frequent and there is a greater use of **enjambement** (running on), where one line flows into the next, seemingly with little or no pause. You will find examples of both in Shylock's speech, Act 1 Scene 3, lines 33–7.

Language and gender

The language of the characters is determined not only by their social class but also partly by their gender. An important question to consider is whether there is a male way of speaking which is different from a female way. Most of the men in the play are preoccupied with matters of finance and the law. The women, though conscious of the importance of wealth, are trapped into hatching love plots on the fringes of male activities. Portia has an interest in the law, but has to resort to dressing up as a man before she can act on behalf of her husband's best friend.

◆ Read through the entirely male Act 1 Scene 1 and collect examples of words connected with business and commerce.

◆ Now read through Act 1 Scene 2 to find the main topic of the women's conversation. Can you find any other important differences between the language of the two scenes? Write an essay setting out your views, with examples, on whether or not you think there is distinctive 'men's language' and 'women's language' in *The Merchant of Venice*.

Shylock's language

Repetition Different forms of linguistic repetition run through the play, contributing to its atmosphere, creation of character and dramatic impact. Three of the most frequently repeated words are 'Jew' and 'Jews' (used nearly seventy times), 'bond' (around forty times) and 'ring' (thirty-seven times). Their repetition is a clear indication of major preoccupations of the play.

Repetition is a distinctive feature of Shylock's speech. His first four speeches in the play (Act 1 Scene 3) reveal his careful, calculating mind: 'Three thousand ducats, well'; 'For three months, well'; 'Antonio shall become bound, well'; 'Three thousand ducats for three months, and Antonio bound'.

Other repetitions reveal different aspects of his personality: his implacable insistence that 'I'll have my bond' (repeated five times in thirteen lines), his anguish at his losses ('My daughter! O my ducats!') and his enthusiastic praise of Portia in the trial scene when he thinks she will award him his bond ('O wise young judge').

◆ Find several examples of Shylock's repetition. Write a few paragraphs about how they increase the dramatic effect of the scenes in which he appears and reveal something about his character.

Shylock and religion Shylock is an outsider and cannot be categorised with either the wealthy or the poor Christians. The content of his language is also markedly different. He disapproves of the Christians' prodigal, extravagant behaviour, preferring a quiet and simple life in keeping with his strict religious faith. These characteristics are reflected in his language, and his adherence to his faith is intensified through the misfortunes and grief that afflict him.

While the Christians refer to the lurid stories of classical mythology, Shylock speaks of Old Testament morality tales. These frequent references to the Bible would have been familiar to many of the Elizabethan audience who, by law, had to attend church regularly.

◆ Collect examples of Shylock's references to the Bible. Consider what effect they may have on a) an Elizabethan and b) a modern audience's reaction to his character.

History and the Jews

Who are the Jews?

Two thousand years ago the Jews were known as Hebrews or Israelites and lived in the part of the world now known as Israel. At that time their land was occupied by the Romans, who at first allowed them religious freedom but later tried to crush the Jewish faith and culture. Such persecution led many Jews to seek new lives in other countries, a process known as the Diaspora (the dispersion of the Jews).

At the time when Shakespeare wrote *The Merchant of Venice* there were still some Jews left in England, although they may have been reluctant to display their faith too conspicuously for fear of retribution. Their presence in England dates back to the time of William the Conqueror, who encouraged them to settle there. They managed and governed their own community but suffered occasional outbursts against them.

The main reason for the tolerance of the Jews was their contribution to the financial well-being of the country. The Christian Church forbade the charging of interest on loans. In addition, there was no facility for the lending of money commercially within society, so a group of comparatively wealthy Jews established themselves as money-lenders, providing a valuable service to society.

Why were the Jews persecuted?

Successful Jews developed into increasingly attractive targets. They were taxed heavily, had their assets seized when they died and paid taxes to the Christian Church. Many were officially exiled as English suspicion and bigotry grew against them. By the thirteenth century they had been forced to wear the humiliating yellow badge that labelled their religious caste. To the medieval and Tudor English, the word 'Jew' was also a label, signifying the stereotype of a shifty profiteer who was not to be trusted.

By Shakespeare's time, the Jews who remained in England probably still adhered to the Jewish faith even though they publicly professed to be Christian converts. Scholars have tried hard, but failed, to identify any individuals who might have provided the original model for Shylock. However, in 1594, two or three years before the first performance of *The Merchant of Venice*, there was a high-profile trial and execution of a Jewish doctor to Queen Elizabeth, Roderigo Lopez. He was accused of attempting to poison the queen. The public interest in the case prompted a hasty revival of a contemporary playwright's work, Christopher Marlowe's *The Jew of Malta*.

In spite of the malicious myths and legends that grew up around the concept of Jewishness, many of them suggesting that Jews were ritual murderers and child sacrificers, Jews resolutely kept up their customs and their religion. They formed tight-knit communities and became known for their intelligence, hard work and business acumen. These qualities often led to their being mistrusted and resented. This was especially the case in Christian countries, where anti-Jewish feeling (anti-Semitism) can still be very strong. The history of the Jews is still marked by terrible hardship and atrocities. You will find that most European countries have past records of crimes against Jews.

The greatest Jewish suffering was endured during the Nazi domination of Europe before and during the Second World War (1939–45). Under the leadership of Adolf Hitler, the Nazis took control of Germany in 1933. They persuaded many Germans that the Jews were responsible for their country's problems. With widespread popular support, the Nazi government conducted a programme of persecution and extermination of Jewish men, women and children in Germany and the other European countries it occupied. Six million Jews lost their lives during this terrible time: the period of history known starkly as the Holocaust. This appalling cruelty began with the casual everyday racism which Shylock also has to endure from the Christians of Venice.

◆ Study the photograph on page 188, taken in the city of Munich in 1933 at the start of the Nazi domination of Germany. The man wearing the placard is a Jewish lawyer, Dr Spiegel. He had asked for police protection against the Nazis. The placard reads: 'I'll never again make any complaints to the police'. What similarities are there between the cases of Shylock and Dr Spiegel?

◆ Research the history of the Jewish community in your own country, or your own town or district. Use your findings as part of an assignment on the social background of the play.

How Shylock is persecuted

Shylock's treatment at the hands of his fellow Venetians is typical of the intolerance suffered by Jews over the centuries. Throughout the play he endures constant verbal abuse:

evil soul	bloody creditor
villain with a smiling cheek	inhuman wretch
misbeliever	unfeeling man
goodly apple rotten at the heart	harsh Jew
cut-throat dog	O be thou damned, inexecrable dog
stranger cur	currish spirit
fiend	wolfish, bloody, starved and
devil	ravenous
faithless Jew	cruel devil
dog Jew	Beg that thou mayst have leave to
old carrion	hang thyself

Work in groups of four or five. One person sits, and the others surround her/him, calling out insults from the list above. If the person in role as Shylock closes her/his eyes or dares wear a blindfold, the intensity of this experience is heightened. Only use volunteers for the Shylock role and for no longer than thirty seconds. Afterwards, talk about how you felt in role as either Shylock or one of his accusers. Then consider the effect of such habitual abuse on Shylock.

The Merchant of Venice in performance

The Merchant of Venice seems to have been a popular play right from the time it was first performed in 1596 or 1597, although very little is known about productions in Shakespeare's time. Audiences who watched it probably had in their minds Christopher Marlowe's hugely successful *The Jew of Malta* and the trial and execution of Dr Lopez (see p. 187), the Jewish doctor who allegedly tried to poison Queen Elizabeth.

The play was virtually neglected throughout the seventeenth century, but in 1701 George Granville reworked the script as *The Jew of Venice*. He rewrote the play, removing most of the minor characters and promoting Shylock to the title role. He cut and rearranged scenes, adding his own lines and a spectacular banquet scene between Antonio, Bassanio and Shylock.

Granville's version thrived for forty years until Shakespeare's own play returned to the stage in 1741. Prior to that time Shylock was probably played as a comic stereotype, with a flaming red beard. But Charles Macklin's Shylock became a terrifying villain, determined on revenge. That conception became the norm until 1814 when Edmund Kean transformed the role.

Kean's Shylock was a sympathetic portrayal, picking up the complexity of his character and highlighting his intelligence, vulnerability and dignity; it set the benchmark for future productions. Although elaborate scenery and costumes were added in attempts to catch the authenticity of Venice and Belmont, it was Shylock who continued to dominate the play. Some productions cut Act 5 completely, ending the play with Shylock's defeat. At the end of the nineteenth century, Henry Irving won acclaim for his tragic portrayal of Shylock's inherent humanity and nobility.

In the twentieth century, theatrical attempts to realise the full complexity of Shakespeare's play were accelerated by the appalling treatment Hitler and the Nazis meted out to the Jews. The Nazis even used Shakespeare as part of their propaganda. In 1943, Baldur von Schirach, the Nazi governor of Vienna, ordered the local theatre to mount a production of *The Merchant of Venice*. The actor Werner Krauf played Shylock as 'loathsome, strange and amazingly horrible, crawling across the stage'. Of course, there is no justification in

Shakespeare's script for such a gross distortion but the terrible crimes that the Nazis committed upon the Jews have made it impossible for any serious stage version after 1945 to perform *The Merchant of Venice* without taking full account of the Holocaust.

Particularly in the closing decades of the twentieth century, and in the twenty-first, productions have been alert to the problematic nature of the play. Productions have tended to move away from very romantic portrayals of Belmont, choosing instead to emphasise the unpleasant social aspects of the play, particularly the brutal intolerance of anti-Semitic Venice. In a number of productions, Shylock is spat upon by the Christians and reviled or assaulted in other ways. In one production he was constantly ridiculed, jostled and beaten. The audience saw street urchins hound and pelt him with stones. The victorious Christians wrestled him to the floor at the end of the trial scene.

'Now, infidel, I have you on the hip.' The Christians delight in tormenting Shylock.

Some portrayals have stressed Shylock's Jewishness and the import-ance of his faith and kinship with his race. Others have marked him as fully assimilated into a world of traders and bankers. The complexity of his relationship with Jessica has been highlighted, variously show-ing how he loves her overwhelmingly and is sharply angered by her betrayal.

Staging the play

The popular image aroused by Venice is of a city of canals, gondolas, bridges and palaces, a city steeped in history and culture. Belmont conjures up visions of a great country house or estate set in expansive grounds, a sophisticated and opulent location.

It was a feature of nineteenth-century productions of *The Merchant of Venice* to use these stereotypical settings, to make the locations as authentic as possible. The sets became ever more spectacular, using splendid painted scenery and architecture to evoke the picturesque world of Venice. The scene below was re-created with remarkable accuracy and attention to detail, reflecting the Victorians' concern for historical realism.

The twentieth century, however, saw a wider range of interpretations. Some productions were deliberately vague and surreal (see p. 28). Others set the play meticulously in the 1880s (showing a Victorian Venice of opulence and materialism) or, particularly, in the 1930s (see the photograph below).

This 1930s Venice has been portrayed as an elegant café society peopled by wealthy Christians in snazzy suits. Blacks (including Lancelot) were shown to have the menial jobs. But it was a world more like 1930s Germany than Italy, and constantly drew on a modern audience's awareness of Nazi oppression and the Holocaust.

◆ Look back at the photographs of previous productions of *The Merchant of Venice*. Identify the staging which you think offers the most interesting dramatic possibilities and explain your choice.
◆ In which period would you set your production of the play? Give reasons for your choice.

The trial scene has inspired striking sets such as the two below.

- Talk together about the staging opportunities offered by the two sets.
- What do you think the set designers intended?

Stage your own production of *The Merchant of Venice*

Talk together about the period and place in which you will set your production. Clearly, any historical setting, particularly one that is post-Holocaust, will have significant resonances. Then choose one or more of the following activities:

- Design the basic set. If your production is going to be school-based, you will need to work with a particular space in mind (either indoors or outdoors). Decide where you want the audience to be seated. Consider whether you want a thrust stage or whether you want to present the play 'in the round'. Sketch your set or make a three-dimensional model of it. Work out how you will use the set to depict the three different locations: Venice, Belmont and the courtroom.
- Design the costumes. Study some of the ways Shylock has been presented (see p. 175). Think about the three disguises needed. Draw contrasting pictures of Portia as herself and then as Doctor Balthazar.
- Design the props. Two important ones are the scales and the knife, used in the trial scene. What about the caskets?
- Design a sound programme to accompany any one scene.
- Design a publicity poster. Use illustrations and language that will make people take notice.
- Design the programme. It could include a summary of the plot, a cast list, interviews with the actors, a history of recent productions and rehearsal photographs.
- Cast the play. Suggest people at your school or college, or from the world of TV, theatre or the media.
- Choose any scene from the play and produce your version of a director's prompt book for that scene. Your prompt book should include detailed notes about the ways in which you want the actors to perform the script, notes on the setting and props, on entrances and exits – anything, in fact, that will help you to bring that scene to life!

Shakespeare's Globe

In Shakespeare's day, Portia, Jessica and other female parts were played by boys, which makes their 'dressing up' as men very ironic! Shylock was probably played as a comic stereotype with a flaming red beard. There were no elaborate sets on the bare stage of the Globe Theatre. Only a few props were used (knife, scales etc.), but the actors wore attractive and expensive costumes, usually the fashionable dress of the times. The Globe Theatre has now been rebuilt on London's Bankside, close to the site on which it first stood. Each year at least one production is staged as Elizabethan audiences probably saw it.

The 1998 production of *The Merchant of Venice* was performed in this 'authentic' style (but with female parts played by females). The picture above was taken at the opening of the performance and shows Commedia dell'arte players entertaining the audience. It is unlikely that such performances were staged in Shakespeare's own Globe, but the style was very popular at the time and would have been a familiar feature of life in Venice of the period.

The rebuilt Globe has an international reputation and sometimes invites visiting companies from overseas to perform there. And for its own 1998 production, the Globe invited the leading German actor Norbert Kentrup to play the part of Shylock. At what line in the play do you think this picture was taken?

William Shakespeare
1564–1616

1564 Born Stratford-upon-Avon, eldest son of John and Mary Shakespeare.

1582 Marries Anne Hathaway of Shottery, near Stratford.

1583 Daughter, Susanna, born.

1585 Twins, son and daughter, Hamnet and Judith, born.

1592 First mention of Shakespeare in London. Robert Greene, another playwright, described Shakespeare as 'an upstart crow beautified with our feathers . . .'. Greene seems to have been jealous of Shakespeare. He mocked Shakespeare's name, calling him 'the only Shake-scene in a country' (presumably because Shakespeare was writing successful plays).

1595 A shareholder in The Lord Chamberlain's Men, an acting company that became extremely popular.

1596 Son Hamnet dies, aged 11.
      Father, John, granted arms (acknowledged as a gentleman).

1597 Buys New Place, the grandest house in Stratford.

1598 Acts in Ben Jonson's *Every Man in His Humour*.

1599 Globe Theatre opens on Bankside. Performances in the open air.

1601 Father, John, dies.

1603 James I grants Shakespeare's company a royal patent: The Lord Chamberlain's Men become The King's Men and play about twelve performances each year at court.

1607 Daughter, Susanna, marries Dr John Hall.

1608 Mother, Mary, dies.

1609 The King's Men begin performing indoors at Blackfriars Theatre.

1610 Probably returns from London to live in Stratford.

1616 Daughter, Judith, marries Thomas Quiney.
      Dies. Buried in Holy Trinity Church, Stratford-upon-Avon.

The plays and poems
(no one knows exactly when he wrote each play)

1589–95 *The Two Gentlemen of Verona, The Taming of the Shrew, First, Second and Third Parts of King Henry VI, Titus Andronicus, King Richard III, The Comedy of Errors, Love's Labour's Lost, A Midsummer Night's Dream, Romeo and Juliet, King Richard II* (and the long poems *Venus and Adonis* and *The Rape of Lucrece*).

1596–9 *King John, The Merchant of Venice, First and Second Parts of King Henry IV, The Merry Wives of Windsor, Much Ado About Nothing, King Henry V, Julius Caesar* (and probably the *Sonnets*).

1600–5 *As You Like It, Hamlet, Twelfth Night, Troilus and Cressida, Measure for Measure, Othello, All's Well That Ends Well, Timon of Athens, King Lear*.

1606–11 *Macbeth, Antony and Cleopatra, Pericles, Coriolanus, The Winter's Tale, Cymbeline, The Tempest*.

1613 *King Henry VIII, The Two Noble Kinsmen* (both probably with John Fletcher).

1623 Shakespeare's plays published as a collection (now called the First Folio).